Imagination in Research
AN ECONOMIST'S VIEW

Imagination

An Economist's View

in Research

by GEORGE W. LADD

IOWA STATE UNIVERSITY PRESS  AMES

GEORGE W. LADD is Professor of Economics, Iowa State University, Ames.

© 1987 Iowa State University Press, Ames, Iowa 50010
All rights reserved

Composed by Iowa State University Press from author-provided disks
Printed in the United States of America

FIRST EDITION, 1987

Library of Congress Cataloging-in-Publication Data

Ladd, George W. (George Wells), 1925–
   Imagination in research.

   1. Research—Methodology.   I. Title.
Q180.55.M4L33   1987   001.4   86–27591
ISBN 0–8138–0987–8

Contents

Preface

THE GENESIS of this book was in my first reading of W. I. B. Beveridge's book *The Art of Scientific Investigation* a quarter-century ago. Publicity and reproducibility of methods and results and agreement on rules are characteristics of science. Reading Beveridge led me to suspect that critical elements in the research process are private, nonreproducible, and not bound by the public rules; that our courses on research methods spend ample time on the interpersonally comparable (and impersonal) and not enough time on the personal and the intrapersonally unique; and that the courses tend to give students a false impression of the research process. Additional reading and observation strengthened my suspicion and slowly led me to realize that the topics on which we spend insufficient time are the ones dealing with innovation. My reading also led me to believe that by covering these topics in a course we can help our students to become more creative scientists. Some have questioned my belief that teachers can do something to increase our students' inventiveness. This book is at once my testimonial to my belief that we can do so and have a responsibility to do so, my evidence to support that belief, and my attempt to act on it.

In February 1979 the *American Journal of Agricultural Economics* published my article "Artistic Research Tools for Scientific Minds," which dealt with some of the same topics as this book. This book quotes liberally without citation from that paper. The profession's generous response to that article encouraged me to learn more and to share what I learned. This book is the result.

Section 1 summarizes the views that led me to write this book. Section 2 shows that the purpose of research reports precludes discussion of unconscious mental processes and chance in them. Following sections present characteristics of unconscious mental processes and introduce Koestler's (1964) concept of bisociation, which he asserts is the essence of creativity. This is followed by a discussion of conscious (primary) mental processes that shows that their nature severely limits their use in the inventive process. Two sections discuss the inventive mental processes and relate the differences between the left and right hemispheres of the human brain to the differences between conscious and unconscious thought. A person can do a number of things to make the unconscious more productive. Several sections are devoted to conditions that stimulate unconscious mental processes. One is devoted to chance. Every scientist knows how important it is to be lucky. Research is a problem-solving process. Psychologists' findings on problem solving are summarized. They help us to understand why chance plays such an important role in research and how to cultivate it. The book closes with some ideas on stimulating students' imaginations.

You can clearly see that this is not a book on scientific method or epistemology. Most writers on these topics deal with such questions as, How do we identify the hypotheses that we will not reject? Which hypotheses are true? This book concerns temporally and logically prior issues, What are the sources of hypotheses? How can we generate more, useful hypotheses?

Many individuals, some identifiable and some not, have contributed to my education on the topics of this book. I am grateful to all of them. Some of the former group are cited in the text. Students and colleagues to whom I am grateful for their contributions are: Bob Holdren, Ronald Raikes, John Miranowski, Wallace Huffman, Daniel Tilley, Karl Fox, Wayne Ostendorf, and Jeffrey Royer. I have presented several seminars on unconscious mental processes, chance, and writing and have always left the seminar room knowing more than when I entered, though sometimes the new knowledge was simply the realization that I needed to learn more about a topic or needed to read another book. Harold Breimeyer, Alan Randall, and Chester Baker read earlier versions of the manuscript. They made a number of valuable suggestions. I am grateful to Shirley Baum for her cheerful and efficient typing of the successive versions of this manuscript and of many others.

The thought has recently struck me that I am a monopolist. Many economists have written on econometrics, economic theory, forecasting, demand theory, and so on and so on. On some topics the number of books and journals is sufficient to make competitive markets; on others, oligopolistic. But this is the only book on unconscious mental processes in economic research. Whether mine is a valuable monopoly remains to be seen. Certainly I look upon monopoly with less disfavor now than formerly.

PART I
The unconscious in invention

SECTION 1 asserts that unconscious mental processes are important research tools but does not attempt to justify the assertion. Sections 2 through 6 explicate the nature of conscious and unconscious mental processes and the stages of scientific invention. These five sections provide evidence to justify my assertion in Section 1.

1 *A neglected research tool*

THE PRIMARY RESEARCH and problem-solving tool is the same in all
sciences: the human mind. All others are derivatives of that one. Our
computers, statistical methods, and theories are all products of the
human mind. But, and here is a challenge to our educational system,
they are not products of that part of the human mind to which we
devote almost all our attention in education: the conscious mind, the
secondary processes, the left hemisphere of the human brain. The
derivative research tools were invented or created. Conscious processes
do play a role in invention, but it is primarily that of critic, not
creator. The source of new inventions, their birthplace if you will, is in
the unconscious, primary, mental processes. And we devote much less
time to helping students develop their unconscious minds than to
developing their conscious minds.

There is a paradox in our education. When we teachers of courses
in research methods select the procedures we want our students to
learn, two criteria we apply are frequency of application and versatil-
ity. But we do not apply them consistently. The research tools that are
most frequently used and most versatile receive little attention in our
courses. I refer to unconscious mental processes (imagination, intuition, hunch), chance, and writing. By our failure to cover these topics
we are providing our students less of an education than we should,
and can, provide them.

Testimony to the usefulness of unconscious mental processes in
research can be found, *inter alia*, in writings by the neurologist Austin
(1978); the animal pathologist Beveridge (1957); the mathematicians
Allendoerfer (1962), Hadamard (1954), and Polya (1957); the biologist Young (1951); the sociologist Porterfield (1941); the economist
Schumpeter (1954, pp. 41–46, 113–14, 124); and the philosophers
Braithwaite (1960, p. 27) and Popper (1959, pp. 31–32; 1962, pp.
28, 352). In a letter Einstein wrote, "When I examine myself and my
methods of thought, I come to the conclusion that the gift of fantasy

has meant more to me than my talent for absorbing positive knowledge" (Clark 1971, p. 87). Testimony on the effects of chance and luck
can be found in the books by Austin, Beveridge, Polya, and Porterfield.

One aim of this book is to explore ways of bringing our practices
in science education into closer conformity with our criteria. The book
is mainly concerned with graduate education in science and is addressed to graduate students. It is also concerned with unconscious
mental processes and more specifically with ways of making them
more productive. Making our unconscious more productive will have a
secondary effect of making our derivative research tools more useful.
Thus this book has a utilitarian purpose. But it also has a recreational
purpose. With the possible exception of psychologists, psychiatrists,
and neurologists, we scientists use our minds to study what is "out
there," to learn what that world out there is like. But it is challenging
and great fun to try to use the mind to understand the mind. And
that is what we will be doing in this book: trying to learn how to
handle the human mind to make the mind more productive.

2 *Research report not a report of research*

WHILE WORKING on their theses, some students are surprised and troubled to find that their research does not proceed in the neat way that journal articles do. The discovery disturbs them and causes them to question their competence. They need not be so concerned. Published research did not proceed as reported either. A journal article is intended to be a presentation of findings, not a history of activity and not an autobiography. Nobel Prize winner Peter Medawar (1967, p. 151) has written that "scientific papers [do] not merely conceal but actively misrepresent the reasoning that goes into the work they describe." Kuhn (1969, Ch. 10) devotes an entire chapter to a similar thesis: that textbooks invariably misrepresent the history of developments in a science. Along this same line, Austin (1978, p. xii) has written, "Experience tells me that research is a series of contingencies, of zigzags, joined by one fragile link after another. You would never realize this from reading the tidy, aseptic research accounts that fill our libraries. For balance, someone should . . . show some contemporary research in all its haphazard, unpredictable complexity." Young (1951) also (though he does not use these same words) refers to the haphazard, unpredictable complexity of the research process.

Allendoerfer (1962, pp. 463–64) has written on the difference between mathematical research and reporting:

It is no wonder that students are baffled by the very idea of doing research in mathematics. . . .

Beginning with nature, . . . we seek to find as many relationships within it as we can. . . . On the basis of what we have observed, we guess theorems and use these to derive other theorems. Immediately we rush to apply these back again to nature and proceed headlong if our predictions are successful. Axioms, logic, and rigor are thrown to the winds, and we become intoxicated with our successes and open to dreadful errors. . . .

It is by this means [intuition] . . . that the great majority of mathematical theorems are first discovered. The products of this intuitive discovery are frequently wrong, usually unorganized, and always speculative. And so there follows the task of sorting them out, weaving them into a proper theory, and proving them on the basis of a set of axioms. It is at this stage that the mathematical model is likely to be constructed. The details of this process go in our seminars and in our discussions . . . , but almost never appear in print. Hence the inner circle of creative mathematicians have the well-kept trade secret that in a great many cases theorems come first and axioms second. This process of justifying a belief by finding premises from which it can be deduced is shockingly similar to much reasoning in our daily lives, and it is somewhat embarrassing to me to realize that mathematicians are experts in this art.

It is easy to understand why scientific papers do not give a true picture of the nature of scientific research and why the research procedure sections of professional journal articles do not discuss the research process. One of Keynes's books was entitled *Essays in Persuasion.* Well, all published research reports are essays in persuasion. Their authors wrote them to persuade some readers of something: to persuade policymakers of the rightness of their answers, to persuade colleagues of the correctness of their new method or the importance of the new problem they have identified, to persuade their deans that they deserve promotion, and so on. A report of the sequence of steps followed to obtain your results is rarely the most persuasive way to report your work. Reporting your haphazard efforts and the unpredictable complexities you encountered and all your zigs and zags, false starts, fruitless ideas, and frustrations does not enhance your credibility and persuasiveness. Neither does it provide readers any evidence they can use to test your argument.

I wish that some great contemporary economist would write an autobiographical report of some of his or her discoveries, as Watson (1968) did. His book recounts the events that led to the discovery of the structure of DNA, a discovery for which he, Francis Crick, and Maurice Wilkins were awarded the Nobel Prize for Medicine and Physiology in 1962. Significantly, the book is subtitled *A Personal Account.* . . . Even a quick reading will vividly demonstrate what I mean by the difference between a report of results and a report of activity.

Deductive reasoning is an excellent tool for persuasion and consequently looms large in research reports. It is more useful for persuasion than for discovery or invention, and consequently it has a more prominent place in research reports than in research processes. The kind of reasoning most prominent in economics research reports is deductive logic: reasoning from assumptions to conclusions. Even when reports present deductive arguments from deductive studies, they can give a misleading picture of the research process. The report presents each step as a necessary and inevitable, even obvious, consequence of preceding steps. The phrase "it obviously follows that consequence C holds" appeared in the mathematics text we used in my undergraduate class in differential equations. At the beginning of a fifty-minute class, a student apologetically asked the instructor to derive the obvious consequence. At the end of the period the instructor was still unable to derive C from the preceding material, but he succeeded in doing so by the next period. It is obvious that consequence C was not obvious to the instructor or to the students. When first discerned by the author of the journal article, the obvious argument and obvious conclusion were quite possibly no more obvious than was consequence C in the textbook to the instructor and the students. It was long after the conclusions were proved that they and their derivations became obvious to the author.

The author of a research report does not tell you how he first came to see the consequences of his assumptions. Anyone who has ever marveled, as I have, at the cleverness of some indirect proof or proof by contradiction must have wondered how the author first came to discover that the result was implied by the assumptions and to discover the indirect proof. Braithwaite (1960, p. 27) wrote of "the mixture of *insight* and trial-and-error" involved in constructing a proof or solving a mathematical problem (emphasis mine).

What insights or what series of trials and errors originally led to the hunch that the theorem is true? And what additional insight or experiment lead to the discovery of the indirect proof?

(I here use "proof" and "theorem" in the sense in which Stoll [1961, p. 125] used them. A proof is a finite sequence of statements of a theory in which each statement is an assumption or is obtained from one or more of the preceding statements by a logical rule of inference. A theorem is the last statement [the conclusion] of a proof. The questions of the logical validity and the truth [factual or material] of a proof are separate questions. "All men have long beards. I am a man. Therefore I have a long beard" is a proof [that is, it is logically valid] of a materially false statement because I shave daily. On the other hand, "All men are clean shaven. I am clean shaven. Therefore I am a man" is logically invalid and therefore not a proof, but its conclusion is true. If a contradiction can be derived as a logically valid

consequence of the statements S_1, S_2, . . . , S_n and the negation of
statement S_{n+1}, this constitutes an indirect proof that statement S_{n+1}
can be derived as a logical consequence of S_1, S_2, . . . , S_n.)

Authors do not tell you how the insights that showed them the
implications of their assumptions or the indirect method of proof
came to them. They do not show you the first 12 proofs attempted,
since they were logically invalid or incomplete. Authors do not tell
you about all the mistakes made in developing the valid proof, even
after insight suggested the general outline, nor about all the consequences discerned early that turned out not to be consequences of the
assumptions. Authors do not tell you that they knew the truth of the
material on page 11 long before they could prove it, that the argument on page 11 was completed six months before the argument on
page 10 even though the argument on page 10 is needed to justify the
argument on page 11. Or perhaps it was not like this at all. Perhaps an
investigator knew the theorem from the very beginning and saw the
theorem and proof in one comprehensive flash of insight. This investigator does not and cannot tell you the foundation of her knowing and
source of her vision; she just knew and saw. She can report the vision,
but not the process that produced it. Or an investigator may have
stumbled across proof and theorem while searching for something
else. All three processes may have contributed elements of the final
product. Because the report will present proof and theorem, but not
the process of discovery, it tells you nothing about the research process, it only tells you the research product. The previous quotation
from Allendoerfer touches on the role of intuition in discovery of
theorems.

Neither does an author of a deductive report tell you where the
assumptions came from. They may be common assumptions justified
by previous writers. But what about the paper with new, or at least
partly new, assumptions? When the author of such a paper devotes
little discussion to the assumptions, what we may have is a deductive
report of a retroductive study. Deduction proceeds from assumptions
to conclusions. According to the standard treatment, retroduction
starts with observation of some regularity and constructs an (hypothesized) explanation of it. A successful retroductive study finds a set of
assumptions, one of whose consequences is the observed regularity. In
deduction, one's initial givens are the assumptions; in retroduction,
the initial given is the observed regularity. Deduction derives the logical implications of assumptions. Retroduction constructs an explana-

tion of something observed. Retroduction involves use of deduction and leads to nothing more than tentative or probable results because every observed regularity that has one explanation has many possible explanations. We can indubitably and finally test each consequence in a deductive argument for validity by applying rules of mathematics or logic. We cannot indubitably and finally establish one explanation of anything observed as being "the true" or "the correct" explanation. See Hanson (1958, Ch. 4) for further discussion of retroduction as the method of reasoning involved in inferring antecedents that have as a logical consequence the observed phenomena.

One thing missing from the deductively organized report of a retroductive study, the absence of which obscures the research process in such studies, is discussion of the source of the hypotheses that produce the explanation. What observations, what insights, what hunches, what plausible inferences finally led to the set of assumptions presented? I write "finally" advisedly because it rarely if ever happens that the first explanations work. They do not explain what you want them to.

A deductively organized report of a retroductive study makes a circular process appear linear. The study started with the observed regularity, went from there to a set of assumptions, and from this to the observed regularity. The report starts with the assumptions. "Circular study" is a deceivingly neat term. Actually the circle has more the configuration of a buzz saw blade with irregular zigs and zags on the circumference. It also has loops, loops within loops, and loops within zigs. The author of a deductive report of a retroductive study tries to convince you that the logical consequences follow from the antecedents in the argument (and they do unless a logical error was made). But the purpose, and the process, of the research was to find antecedents that yielded a particular logical consequence: the observed regularity that started it all. A retroductive study also yields hypotheses that explain other regularities: some not even observed yet and some perhaps observed but not previously understood.

I have discussed retroduction in conventional terms, that is, as starting from an observed regularity. We must ask, How did one happen to notice the regularity in the absence of any reason to suspect its existence? Normally, unexpected regularities do not force themselves upon our attention. How did this unexpected regularity make itself noticed? Chance may have played a role. A likely answer is that it was not unexpected. The investigator intuited, guessed, or hoped for a regularity, then either (1) behaved as if he or she had observed it, found an explanation, and submitted the explanation to test or (2) tested the guess, found it verified, and derived an explanation. From the published report you cannot tell whether the investigator started with an observed regularity or with a hunch. We might call items 1 and 2 "prayerful retroduction."

Retroductive thinking is more difficult than deductive thinking because it requires the latter and, in addition, requires finding (or imagining or intuiting) assumptions that imply (through deductive logic) the existence of the phenomenon you wish to explain. Your assumptions may be beyond criticism and your logic impeccable, but you may still fail to account for the observed phenomenon that you want to explain. Or you may find an explanation of one phenomenon that is inconsistent with other observations.

How many times have you read a research report that follows a one-page statement of problem and objectives with a half-page discussion on "we developed a questionnaire" and then devotes eight pages to discussion of empirical work and results? Does not such a report give you the impression that the important thing was the empirical work and that was where the hard work went? A ratio of one-half page on questionnaire to eight pages on empirical study gives a misleading impression on relative allocation of resources and the nature of the research process. In some studies the number of person-years devoted to questionnaire construction greatly, and necessarily, exceeds the number devoted to empirical analysis. Computer scientists write of the GIGO Principle (garbage in = garbage out) to emphasize that computer output is no better than the input. If unreliable or biased data go in, unreliable or biased results come out. This principle must be kept firmly in mind when constructing and using a questionnaire. Because of the low ratio of number of pages on questionnaire to number on statistical results, published studies hide the actual process followed in carrying out the study. A computer scientist tells me of a more recent interpretation of GIGO that expresses concern over excessive faith in computer output: garbage in = gospel out.

In some reports, a ratio of one page of problem statement to eight pages of results and analysis grossly understates the proportion of time devoted to problem formulation. In many studies, problem formulation is the most mentally demanding and difficult part of the study; the empirical analysis can be done almost mechanically after the problem is properly formulated. Few authors devote any time to justifying their choice of problem formulation over alternative formulations.

It is worth pondering the significance of the title of Beveridge's (1957) book, *The Art of Scientific Investigation,* not the "Science of Scientific Investigation." Scientific research is an activity, a doing: an art. Science is organized knowledge. And activity is not knowledge, though it may lead to knowledge and may appear (and may be) unorganized.

To round out this discussion, some other points should be mentioned. First, research reports are supposed to focus on the investigation, not on the investigator. Investigators who write about all the things that "we did" or "were attempted" soon feel that they are spending too much time writing about themselves. Second, students are taught that reproducibility is an essential element of science. But unconscious mental processes are not reproducible. When those students become researchers, they remember their lessons and do not report their nonreproducible experiences. Third, people fear that admitting that "I stumbled across a solution" may not give their deans the confidence they must have in them to recommend their promotion.

3 *Some characteristics of*
unconscious mental processes

HAVE YOU EVER had an experience like this? You are involved in a discussion and making a point that requires you to talk for, say, two minutes. Halfway through you become conscious of a useful, relevant idea, but by the time you complete the two minutes of talk you have lost the idea. And you are unable to remember or re-create the idea no matter how hard you try.

What happened was that your unconscious mental processes created a suggestion and put it forward for your conscious to catch and evaluate, and your conscious processes failed to catch and hold the idea. This is typical of unconscious processes. They create ideas, concepts, thoughts, and relationships for the conscious mental processes to catch and evaluate. The conscious thought processes have to be prepared to catch these suggestions because they often appear at the fringe of consciousness rather than at the center.

In a comic strip, Mr. Born Loser is walking along mumbling to himself, "Backward, turn backward, oh time in thy flight, I just thought of a comeback I needed last night." Perhaps this has happened to you. An hour, a day, even a week after a discussion or argument, a good idea occurs to you that would have won your case. Here your unconscious processes continued to mull over a situation after your conscious processes had shifted to another problem, and your unconscious mental activities produced an idea they threw out to your conscious.

The term "unconscious" describes mental processes such as thoughts, ideas, and feelings that occur in our minds without our being aware of them. Freud's comparison of the human mind to an iceberg illustrates the view of the unconscious held by many psychologists and psychiatrists. Only one-eighth of an iceberg is visible above the water; the remaining seven-eighths is below the surface. Only a small fraction of our mental processes are conscious, above the surface of consciousness. A large fraction are below the surface, unconscious (or subconscious) processes.

It is proper to write of conscious and unconscious thoughts, processes, activities, and results. It is not strictly proper to differentiate unconscious and conscious mind, suggesting as it does the possession of two minds within each human brain. The proper distinction is not between the conscious and unconscious mind but between levels of awareness in one mind. I will, however, primarily for brevity and convenience, write of the conscious mind and the unconscious mind or even of the conscious and unconscious in place of "conscious mental processes" and "unconscious mental processes."

The term "unconscious" does not usually have the same meaning in "unconscious person" and "unconscious processes." The first phrase sometimes means "knocked out," as from a kick in the head. Following Jaynes (1977, pp. 21–23), we can say that a person who has been knocked out lacks consciousness and also lacks reactivity. But an "unconscious person" may be a "sleeping person." A sleeping person does not lack reactivity but can react to external stimuli. Unconscious mental processes can take place in both unconscious and conscious persons. Consciousness is not necessary for reactivity. If you walk over broken ground you continually react to effects of gravity by leaning forward as you climb, leaning back as you descend, and walking vertically on level spots, without being aware that you are adjusting your posture.

Unconscious mental processes are not like unconscious physiological processes such as respiration, blood circulation, or digestion. If healthy, we can count on our bodies to carry out the physiological processes automatically without any conscious direction from us. We cannot similarly count on our unconscious to provide new ideas automatically, whenever they might be useful, without any conscious direction from us. We can, however, consciously take various steps that increase the frequency with which our unconscious will provide useful ideas.

Hadamard (1954, p. 23) uses a familiar comparison to illustrate an important difference between the conscious and the unconscious:

Identifying a person you know requires the help of hundreds of features, not a single one of which you could explicitly mention (if not especially gifted or trained for drawing). Nevertheless, all these characters of the face of your friend must be present in your mind — in your unconscious mind, of course — and all of them must be present at the same instant. . . . The unconscious has the important property of being manifold; several and probably many things can and do occur in it simultaneously. This contrasts with the conscious ego which is unique.

Normally, we are not aware of the unconscious operations because the results combine with our conscious thoughts to provide an orderly, reasonable, ordinary stream of consciousness. It is only when the unconscious efforts present a new, exciting, extraordinary thought that we are made aware of their operation or when they present a thought on a topic other than the one we are consciously pondering.

The unconscious processes provide raw materials that our conscious processes use. Many of our conscious ideas, concepts, and thoughts originate in the unconscious processes, and the unconscious throws them up for conscious evaluation. Conscious processes, if you will, wait upon the unconscious to give them something to do. A person known as being quick-witted has an unconscious that is quick to respond to stimuli and to respond in an appropriate manner.

In problem solving (and doing research requires solving problems) the unconscious and the conscious form a team. The recognition of a problem provides a stimulus. We hope the unconscious will then generate a possible solution and push it into the conscious mind. Then the conscious mind enters the problem-solving process. Reason is used to examine and accept or reject the proposed solution. If it is rejected, the conscious mind waits until the unconscious suggests a new solution. Then conscious reason comes into play again. Solutions originate in unconscious mental processes. Some of these will turn out upon conscious examination not to be solutions at all or to be bad or incomplete. A job of the conscious mind is to evaluate the various solutions proposed by the unconscious. Some solutions may originate in the conscious. It seems likely that these are derivatives obtained while one is consciously examining and modifying ideas that originated in the unconscious.

Given Freud's comparison of the mind to an iceberg and given that ideas often originate in the unconscious, it is desirable to increase its productivity. Fortunately, you can do various things to stimulate the unconscious because it does respond to stimuli. And you can exercise some control over the amount, variety, and strength of the stimuli your unconscious receives. By controlling these stimuli, you exercise some control, although rather loose and permissive, over your unconscious; however, this is not enough. It is necessary to sensitize your conscious mind to the operations of the unconscious to minimize the number of ideas that are created by the unconscious and lost before they penetrate the conscious. Some of the things you do to stimulate your unconscious to create ideas also stimulate your conscious to grasp them. Things you can do to stimulate the operations of the unconscious will be presented later.

A person will speak of "an idea that I had." This phrase suggests a willful, voluntary act performed by that person. But we cannot will our unconscious minds to act; neither can we strictly control them. Having unconscious ideas is not something we deliberately and willfully do; it is something done for us or to us by our unconscious minds in response to stimulation. Instead of speaking of "an idea that I had," it would be more appropriate to speak of "an idea my unconscious generated in response to stimuli." I may have provided the stimuli, or someone else may have provided them.

Most of the ideas generated by our unconscious processes turn out, upon evaluation by our conscious mental processes, to be useless, or at least inapplicable in the context in which they came to mind. This does not mean, however, that we must refuse to rely on our unconscious minds because they are often wrong. It means exactly the contrary. Because unconscious minds are often wrong, to increase their usefulness we must have more ideas, knowing that a large proportion of them will be bad. And we must use our conscious minds to discriminate. The unconscious generates ideas; the conscious evaluates them.

We must understand that unconscious mental processes are not the lazy mind's way of thinking. A lazy mind's unconscious is no more active nor productive than its conscious. The reasons are many; they are found scattered throughout Parts II and IV. One obvious reason is that hard conscious effort must precede fruitful unconscious effort.

Imagination and intuition. Psychologists speak of several kinds of imagination. Daydreams and nightdreams are instances of passive imagination. Reproductive imagination is the capacity to form mental pictures of past experiences. The kind of imagination of most concern in science is productive or creative. Senator Robert F. Kennedy is reported to have said, "Some people see things as they are and wonder why. I see things that never were and ask why not?" To see things that never were is an act of creative imagination. This type of imagination involves taking bits of experience and putting them together into new forms. The new form is an invention. The invention may be something physical like the telephone or the electric light. It may be an artistic piece. It may be a new concept, new idea, or new model. Frequently, in research the product of the imagination is a link between things that were not formerly seen to be connected in any way. "A thing learned in certain connections is torn out of the context in which it was learned, for use in some new context" (Guilford 1967, p. 100).

Porterfield (1941, p. 62) refers to the association and dissociation of mental items. Ideas, facts, relationships, or concepts become dissociated from their previous contacts and become associated together in new ways. It is not true that "there is nothing new under the sun." Every one of these links is something new. Porterfield also discusses synopsis and synthesis as processes of imagination. Synopsis or "whole-sight" provides a view of the whole of a problem or situation. Synthesis provides understanding of relations among the parts of the whole. Hadamard argues that the act of synthesis is performed in the unconscious rather than in the conscious because of the manifold character of the former and the uniqueness of the latter.

Poincare (1913) explains the obvious fact that not everyone can understand mathematical reasoning. The difference that he sees between the person who can and one who cannot understand is a matter of difference in intuition. The one who understands the argument has a feeling or an intuition for the argument as a whole and for the progression of its elements and can intuitively synthesize the argument. The one who fails to understand lacks this feeling, even though he or she may understand each individual step.

Creative imagination has been responsible for the masterpieces of the arts; for tools and machines; for models, theories, and concepts. In discussing creative imagination, Weld (1956, p. 707) wrote:

In constructive imagination . . . the successive ideas not only have a direction, but they also drive forward to an end, namely the new creation. The determining factors here are dispositions in the nervous system which may or may not find conscious representation. In the first place we have . . . "the instinct of creation, the need of producing in a determined line." This, if mentally expressed, comes as a vague ambition or aim, and the disposition serves to restrict all ideas that do not fit in with the ambition or aim. Then, without warning but usually after long incubation and as the result of some chance situation, or some grouping of associative tendencies, a new meaning, a happy thought, is born. . . . In view of the suddenness of its initiation, its unaccountableness, its feeling of strangeness and the joy which it sometimes brings, the new idea often seems to come as an inspiration from on high. Sometimes the new conception comes in its complete form. . . . But at other times and more frequently, the new idea is vague, incomplete or only in outline and the period that follows is one of hard labor characterized by secondary attention, conflicting ideas and variable moods.

The terms used by Weld (suddenness, unaccountableness, strangeness, joy, inspiration) are sometimes used to describe intuition. In philosophy, intuition is immediate knowledge attained without conscious deliberation or reasoning. In the theory of knowledge, intuition is the immediate apprehension of truth. It is "knowing without knowing why I know." Beveridge (1957, p. 91) defines it as "a sudden enlightenment or comprehension of a situation, a clarifying idea which springs into the consciousness, often, though not necessarily, when one is not consciously thinking of the subject."

We all have these intuitions or sudden insights. What many people do not realize is their great importance to scientific research. Also, many do not realize that they are a research tool, just as linear programming or least squares, and the unconscious mental processes that create them can be stimulated to be more productive.

Bisociation. As stated earlier, a product of the creative imagination is frequently a link between things that were not previously connected in any way. So important is this product that Koestler coined a special name for it: bisociation. Associations relate things to each other in the same frame of reference, universe of discourse, or plane of experience. A bisociation connects things from two different frames of reference, universes of discourse, or planes of experience. Koestler (1964, p. 38) applies the term "matrix" to a frame of reference, universe of discourse, plane of experience, associative context, or type of logic to "denote any ability, habit, or skill, any pattern of ordered behavior governed by a 'code' of fixed rules." Matrix, code, and strategy describe three aspects of the same thing. The code is fixed, invariable; a matrix is flexible, its use depending on the circumstances; strategy is a choice of actions or ideas. In chess, the rules are the code, the matrix is the total of all possible moves, the strategy is the choice of moves. In the matrix of linear programming the code is provided by the mathematics of linear inequalities. All applications of linear programming are subject to this same code; the variety of applications represents the flexibility of the linear programming matrix.

Most thinking is associative, in which one's thoughts remain in one matrix. Creative thought, Koestler argues, consists of bisociative thinking or bisociation, in which a situation, idea, thing, or concept until now viewed as belonging to one matrix is perceived as belonging to two separate matrices. If the bisociation proves useful, a new synthesis is born; two matrices that were previously separate are transformed and joined to form a new matrix. Koestler maintains that the creative act or idea in humor, art, and scientific discovery consists of a bisociation between two habitually incompatible matrices.

Every human infant goes through a bisociative step when it realizes that things have names and bisociates the two previously unrelated matrices of "sounds" and "things." It has then taken the first steps toward learning to talk.

Bisociation enters into not only the creation of art but also its enjoyment, as Koestler also maintains. When listening to Aaron Copland's composition "Quiet City" causes one to visualize city streets in the early morning hours where the only signs of life are a few scattered lights, an occasional night watchman, and an occasional train whistle or ambulance siren piercing the dark silence, one is bisociating. Two different matrices, one aural and the other visual, momentarily fuse into a unity. If listening to Respighi's "Pines of Rome" evokes a mental image of a Roman legion marching on a stone road past a sun-drenched, pine-covered hillside, bisociation is occurring.

Bisociation makes it possible for us to watch flickering shadows on a movie or TV screen and to admire the acting on the one hand and on the other to endow the shadows with life and care what happens to the people represented by the shadows. The imagination allows us to experience the same shadows on two separate planes of existence.

An example of a failure to bisociate was provided by some master's theses that I read. In each thesis the student dealt quantitatively with some problem facing a multiproduct firm. In discussing theory of the multiproduct firm, the student presented it just as it is presented in the first graduate course in economic theory: based on the classical assumption of a continuous production function with continuous first- and second-order derivatives, the smooth equal-output and equal-input curves were drawn and discussed. In the chapter on quantitative procedure, the student discussed linear programming, just as it was taught in a quantitative methods course. The student had learned to use the classical assumption for theoretical analysis and to use the linear programming assumptions for empirical work but failed to recognize that we can use the linear programming assumptions to develop a theory of the multiproduct firm. The student saw linear programming as a computational tool and failed to bisociate it and firm theory.

In his influential, stimulating, and much discussed book on the history of science, Kuhn conceived of scientific progress as a sequence of scientific revolutions. He wrote (1969, p. 208; emphasis mine):

To the extent that the book portrays scientific development as a succession of tradition-bound periods punctuated by non-cumulative breaks, its theses are undoubtedly of wide applicability. But they should be, *for they are borrowed from other fields*. Historians of literature, of music, of the arts, of political development, and of many other human activities have long described their subjects in the same way. Periodization in terms of revolutionary breaks in style, taste, and institutional structure have been among their standard tools. If I have been original with respect to concepts like these, it has mainly been by applying them to the sciences, fields which had been widely thought to develop in a different way.

Kuhn claims his main originality to have been in using the idea of revolutionary breaks to form a bisociation (although he does not use this term) between history of science and histories of many other human activities. Koestler (1964, Ch. 10) presents essentially the same theses as Kuhn and treats the revolutionary breaks as bisociations.

One effect of the formation of a fruitful bisociation is a change in our mental landscape or mind-set. Some of our matrices and codes are different and we see a part of the world differently. Many of the associations taught in courses in science originated as a bisociation in the mind of one person.

Koestler's idea that every new creation is a bisociation of two existing things is not a depreciation of the value of ingenuity in the creative act. It is a restatement of a well-recognized property of the human mind: an a priori of human thought. It is a fundamental characteristic of the human mind that it cannot conceive of absolute nothing. It can conceive of the absence of autos, air, or people, but it cannot conceive of the absence of everything. Everything has a predecessor, which was something, and has a successor, which is also something. The human mind cannot conceive of the creation of something from nothing nor of the destruction of anything into nothing. Koestler's bisociation is a methodological corollary of the methodological imperative of nonnothingness.

I have called the product of the creative imagination a "link between things not formerly seen to be connected." Koestler's bisociation connotes to me more precisely the nature of many inventions than do the terms "link" or "connection," which suggest tying together things that still retain their separate identities. Usually a bisociation connects two things so intimately that they become parts of a new synthesized whole while still retaining the separate identities they had previously.

Before proceeding, I want to draw a distinction (vague but important) between invention (innovation, creation) on the one hand and novelty on the other. Not everything new is an invention (innovation, creation). The new may only be novel. Just as literature has redeeming social value but pornography does not, so invention has scientific value, but novelty does not. If novelty had value, every student who gives a new wrong answer to a question would get an A grade. A novelty can fail to be an invention for any of a number of reasons: it is contradicted by experience; it fails to explain phenomena as well as an existing explanation does; it solves an insignificant problem. This essay is intended to foster invention, not novelty.

The unconscious and bisociations in economics. In Section 1, I cited a number of authors who testify to the importance of unconscious mental processes. Wiener's (1956, p. 72) first stage in the inductive research process is "the imagination of a theory to fit the facts." In his introduction to Raaheim's book (1974, p. 13) Hunter wrote that "science begins in an act of *imagination*" (emphasis mine). Even philosophers of science acknowledge the importance of unconscious mental processes in research. See, for example, Braithwaite (1960, p. 27) and Popper (1959, pp. 31, 32; 1962, pp. 28, 352).

A number of economists have written on the importance of intuition in economic research. In discussing Keynes's *General Theory* (1936), Hicks (1950, p. 4) wrote:

I must confess that, as I have worked with Mr. Keynes's book, I have been amazed at the way he manages, without the use of any special apparatus, to cut through the tangle of difficulties that beset him, and to go straight for the really important things. He succeeds in doing so just because he makes free use of his superb intuition and acute observation of the real world, in order to be able to discard the inessentials and go straight for the essentials.

Keynes (1963, p. 190) himself had a lively appreciation of the value of intuition. He wrote about Alfred Marshall:

But it was an essential truth to which Marshall held firmly, that those individuals who are endowed with a special genius for the subject and have a powerful economic intuition will often be more right in their conclusions and implicit presumptions than in their explanations and explicit statements. That is to say, their intuitions will be in advance of their analysis and their terminology. . . . Marshall's own economic intuition was extraordinary. . . .

In the same book Keynes also writes admiringly of Frank Ramsey's "intuitive imagination" and Newton's "pre-eminently extraordinary" intuition. Tintner (1974) observed that "the [economics] classics have frequently anticipated with incredibly sharp intuition results in pure economic theory that have been proved only very recently with the help of mathematical methods unknown even to the mathematicians at the time of the classics." Baumol (1985) makes a similar observation. I wonder whether our generation of economists is as wise as the generations that Tintner refers to. Can we intuit profound results that will not be proven for several years? Or can we only know things that we can prove by demonstrative logic?

Schumpeter (1954, pp. 113–14) wrote that "precisely the strongest achievements in science proceed not from observation or experiment and orderly logic-chopping but from something that is best called vision and is akin to artistic creation." His term "strongest achievements" should be interpreted in two distinct but related ways. One is the greatest achievements of a science. The second is the strongest achievements of an individual. The second interpretation needs to be mentioned because many of us do not expect (although we may hope) to make great contributions to our discipline. People who do not expect to make great contributions and think only of the first interpretation may say to themselves, "I'll never make great contributions so I don't need artistic or inventive ability." But if they accept the second interpretation, they can sensibly say, "Learning to increase my creative ability is worthwhile because it will enable me to have more good ideas and to accomplish more than I could otherwise." And the total of a large number of modest contributions can amount to a great deal. A good idea, whether modest or great, brings personal satisfaction to the innovator.

One finds a number of fruitful bisociations in the history of economics. A few will be mentioned here. One bisociation was formed when Quesnay, a physician in the court of Louis XV, applied the newly discovered fact of blood circulation to economics and devised the *tableau économique*. The prevailing view of that day was that wealth consisted of gold and silver. Quesnay argued that wealth sprang from production and flowed through the economy like blood through the body. Marx's dialectical materialism was a bisociation of Hegelian dialectic philosophy and social studies. According to Hegel, change is the rule of life. Every thesis breeds its antithesis and the two merge into a synthesis, which in turn produces its own antithesis. Marx formed the bisociation between this philosophy and history. Skipping ahead several decades, we find Samuelson in his *Foundations* arguing that the theory of the utility-maximizing consumer and the theory of the profit-maximizing competitive firm are not two separate matrices; each is an application of the mathematics of constrained optimization. He wrote (1965, p. 23) that "the study of maximizing behavior affords a unified approach to wide areas of current and historical economic thought." Muth (1966) drew an analogy between households and firms to develop production models of household behavior. Lancaster (1971) bisociated activity analysis and consumer behavior. We all know something of evolution theory. Few economists are aware of the key role that the work of one of their own, Malthus, played in the development of this theory. Malthus's *An Essay on the Principle of Population As It Affects the Future Improvement of Society* suggested the ideas of natural selection to Darwin and of survival of the fittest to Wallace, two key concepts in their development of evolution. See Koestler (1964, pp. 131–44) for details.

 4   *Mental processes*

WHY MUST WE RELY on the unconscious for our new ideas? What are the characteristics of conscious and unconscious thought that allow the latter to be the source of our new ideas? These questions are the concern of this section.

Code as restrictions. A "code" (Koestler's term) is usually thought of as defining a set of permissible actions. Education seeks to teach the codes. A code is also a list of prohibited actions, which are usually implied by being excluded from the list of permissible actions. The rule of calculus, for example, that allows the equation $d(ax + bx^2)/dx = a + 2bx$ also prohibits the equation $d(ax + bx^2)/dx = 2a + bx$ and prohibits a great number of other relations. For every one action permitted by a code, a multitude are prohibited. The prohibitory nature of a code has important implications. Our conscious thought (associative thinking) is ruled by these codes. The operations of the conscious mind represent order, rigor, and pattern: the established system of the codes. The established patterns of our conscious minds determine how we perceive and understand our world. And they determine our behavior. Everything new represents, even if only in a minor way, a departure from the established system of our conscious minds. If we treat as valid only those thoughts that satisfy the rules of conscious thinking, or if we allow ourselves to be aware only of such thoughts, either the unconscious cannot violate the rules to come up with any departure from that system or the conscious refuses to let itself be aware of such departures. A complete and perfect adherence to the existing system of knowledge is a trait, not of the innovator, but of the imitator.

If associative thinking has failed to solve a problem, it is time to try to surmount, violate, or forget the prohibitions of the codes or to relax or modify them. This calls for unconscious thinking because the unconscious is not bound by the codes. It can ignore or forget them and "see things that never were." For example, dreams are a product of the unconscious and they certainly violate codes, for example, those expressed in physical and chemical laws, legislative laws, public morals, and personal habits. In a dream you can stand on a lakeshore and watch yourself fall out of a boat and drown; you can fall from an airplane and land unhurt; you can go to last Saturday's football game with a long-dead parent. In a dream an automobile can be flown into O'Hare airport and taxied to the terminal building. In a dream nothing is impossible.

Some codes become so deeply settled into the unconscious that we do not even realize they are there and we are bound by them. Some of these codes are habits; some are implicit assumptions. They are so much a part of us we cannot even realize there can be anything else. At least we do not realize it until some bisociative shock shows their presence by violating one of them.

I am not suggesting that all conscious thought is orderly and error-free. We know better. Part of our conscious thought is an effort to assure that our conscious output is systematic and error-free. The simple fact that we can acknowledge error in conscious thought is evidence of the existence of rules that must be satisfied for the thoughts to receive acceptance in the scientific community. If all conscious thought were error-free, we would not need rules of logic.

Primary processes: code-free thought. Here we briefly cover processes that are not bound by the codes. Psychologists, following Freud, distinguish primary from secondary mental processes. In writing about code, matrix, frame, associative thinking, and deductive logic, we are dealing with secondary processes. The secondary process is the way the mind thinks when it is awake and using ordinary logical thinking. The primary processes are free from the conscious codes. Why is this so? Part of the answer is found in psycho-history and part in human phylogeny. Jaynes (1977) draws on psychology, neurology, archaeology, and ancient literature to buttress his argument that consciousness (being conscious of what we are conscious of) is a relatively recent development, that the human race has had a consciousness for only roughly 2,500 to 3,000 years.

Arieti (1976, pp. 401) writes:

Biological creativity is evident in many examples offered by the phylogeny of the central nervous system. When new nervous structures emerge as a result of series of mutations and take over some functions from lower structures, these lower structures—what, at a psychological level correspond to our obsolete, archaic, or primary-process mechanisms—are not eliminated. Instead they are readjusted and reintegrated to form a functional system within the higher structure.

The structures in which the primary-process mechanisms occur existed before the codes that govern our conscious thinking in western cultures were developed and codified. These structures have not disappeared, nor have their mental processes. These primitive mental processes are still available to us if we cultivate them, though they seem to be more available to some people than to others.

Arieti (1976) discusses three primary processes. One primitive mental process is imagery: the process of producing and experiencing images, which are connected with past perceptions. They are fleeting; they occur spontaneously but can be encouraged by inactivity and lack of external stimuli. They undergo alterations. Most images rapidly associate with or suggest other images. These last two characteristics make it possible for imagery to create something that did not exist before.

There is abundant evidence on the use of imagery in creative work. Hadamard queried eminent mathematicians in America on their working methods. Summing his results, Hadamard (1954, pp. 83–85) wrote:

Among the mathematicians born or resident in America, . . . phenomena are mostly analogous to those which I have noticed in my own case. Practically all of them . . . avoid not only the use of mental words, but also, just as I do, the mental use of algebraic or any other precise signs; also as in my case, they use vague images. . . . The mental pictures . . . are most frequently visual, but they may also be of another kind, for instance, kinetic. There can also be auditive ones, but even these . . . quite generally keep their vague character.

Nearly a fourth of Hadamard's book (most of Ch. 6) is devoted to imagery. He writes of wordless thought, shows that many eminent scientists do not think in words, and asserts that he does not ever use words or algebraic signs when "really thinking." Words are not used until the stage of communicating or recording results is reached. Some individuals experience visual images; some, kinetic; some, auditory.

The one feature that is common to all is the vagueness of the images. The vagueness is necessary for the images "to lead me without misleading me" (Hadamard 1954, p. 79). The images are fully in the conscious mind. The corresponding thoughts, he argues, are in the fringe consciousness—that part of the unconscious on the edge of consciousness and from which ideas are easily brought into the conscious as they are summoned. Hadamard also reports one awkward consequence of the use of wordless thought that shows up when the time comes to record one's work. The images must be translated into words, but words may be inadequate for expressing them. Even if exact verbal translations do exist, finding them is time consuming. In Hutchinson (1949) evidence can also be found on usefulness of imagery in invention. Koestler (1964), too, discusses imagery (p. 169), visual thinking (p. 183), and images (pp. 322–25) as precursors of conscious thought.

Arieti hypothesizes that another of the primary process functions is what he calls the endocept, which others have called nonverbal, unconscious, or preconscious cognition. "The endocept is a primitive organization of past experiences, perceptions, memory traces, and images of things and movements" (Arieti 1976, p. 54). Endocepts are not expressed in images, words, thoughts, or actions. They remain internal and unexpressed and are largely repressed in adults. Their content is unplanned but is affected by one's previous life history. In the incubation stage of the inventive process, there may be a good deal of endoceptual activity. As long as an endocept remains an endocept, it contributes nothing to creativity. But endocepts may be transformed into symbols, actions, images, definite feelings, or dreams or fantasies. Any of these transformations, if they penetrate the conscious, may lead to or become part of a creative product. When an endocept is suddenly transformed into a conscious thought, we speak of it as an intuition.

A third type of primary process thinking, variously called primitive, archaic, or obsolete, is labeled "paleologic" by Arieti (1976, Ch. 5). Unlike imagery and endoceptual cognition, but like secondary processes, paleologic thinking does use words and ideas. It is sensitive to similarities and capable of dividing wholes into discernible parts. Consequently, paleologic thinking can create classes (or sets or groups) that the conscious would never perceive or conceive. Such classes consist of objects that share a single (or a few) common characteristic. A single item may have a large number of characteristics. Thus the possibilities for novel paleologic classes are enormous. In addition, in paleologic thinking the members of a class are viewed as equivalent; similarity and identity are not distinguished. This sort of thinking allows things that are unthinkable in conscious reasoning. It permits violation of the law of identity by allowing A to become (or be) B, that is, to become not A. It permits violation of the law of the excluded middle by allowing something to be neither A nor not A. Ability to form classes based on a single characteristic and to violate the laws of identity and the excluded middle allows paleologic thinking to discover new similarities, analogies, or identities that the conscious would not see but that can lead to a creative product.

Under conscious examination the similarities discovered by paleologic thinking may be the basis for identifying a completely new class of items or a new concept. This newly discovered similarity between two things may turn out to be a similarity that characterizes relationships among a large number. The concept of a class or a set is a powerful investigative tool because each new item that is identified as belonging to the class possesses the attributes possessed by those items already in it.

Paleologic thinking also tends to give concrete form to abstractions. Poets and painters use paleologic thinking in transforming abstractions into concrete images.

To Freud's primary and secondary processes, Arieti adds tertiary ones to denote combinations of the primary and secondary or combinations of normal and faulty secondary processes that contribute to creativity.

One hallmark of creative minds is a relatively free flow of messages between the conscious and unconscious, between the primary and secondary processes. In Section 3 I wrote that the unconscious generates ideas and the conscious evaluates them. This is too simple a description. Poincare (1913, pp. 390–92), for one, has argued that the unconscious does a good deal of discriminating. And it is clear that the unconscious receives guidance and stimulus from the conscious. The conscious evaluation activity involves much more than simply accepting or rejecting ideas. It also involves modifying them to make a coherent whole, relating them to conscious knowledge, identifying gaps, locating inconsistencies, searching for the link that justifies the unconscious association of A with B, and probably identifying potentially fruitful avenues for filling the gaps or eliminating the inconsistencies. The bisociations or similarities generated by the unconscious may be modified by the conscious.

In great creative minds the communication among the various levels of the mind must be wonderfully intimate and remarkably delicate. Each level must be sensitive to the results of the others and must appreciate the value of the method by which the others work, while freely operating in its own way. If the conscious imposes its rules upon the operations of the unconscious, the result is mimicry not creativity. If the unconscious imposes its will upon the conscious, the result is chaos. There is no limit to the damage that the unconscious can do if it is turned loose.

The images that Einstein, Hadamard, and Hutchinson wrote about were communicated to their conscious mental processes. Repression of imagery is a common phenomenon. One must wonder why the repression of images is common if imagery is common. Psychologists and psychiatrists have written on this. I suspect that a force leading to the repression is one they have not treated. The repression is partly due to our failure as teachers to show students that unconscious mental processes are as valid and valuable as conscious processes and that "we are a great deal wiser than our intellect, and, unfortunately a great many people don't recognize that, particularly intellectuals such as college professors. . . . And I cannot be aware of how much we possess of a much greater range of wisdom" (MacKinnon 1966, p. 189). The truth that MacKinnon expresses was recognized long ago by the poet who wrote, "The heart has reasons that the mind knows not." Note also that the philosophers Nagel and Newman (1960, p. 101) wrote that Gödel's theorem means that "the resources of the human intellect have not been, and cannot be, fully formalized. . . ."

MacKinnon's assertion of our unawareness of our greater range of wisdom provides an introduction to our next topic (left brain–right brain). Understanding the different methods of operation of the brain's two hemispheres helps in understanding how we can know more than we can be aware of. And it also provides insight into the mind's different methods of thinking.

Hemispheral lateralization. Sometimes a person who cannot decide on an answer or action will say, "I am of two minds about that." The person would probably be literally correct in saying, "I am of two hemispheres about that" because the left and right hemispheres of the human brain do work differently and can come up with different answers. I will summarize differences that psychologists, psychiatrists, and neurologists have found. (LH means left hemisphere and RH means right hemisphere.)

In the great majority of people we find the following differences. This summary is based on Austin (1978), Hansen (1981), Jaynes (1977), Springer and Deutsch (1981), and Wittrock (1977):

1. LH processes information analytically; RH processes it synthetically. LH abstracts details and associates them with verbal symbols; RH is more concerned with relationships of parts to wholes, with Gestalt formation. Austin (1978, p. 139) picturesquely describes the analytic-synthetic dichotomy: "While its left partner proceeds, piecemeal, to examine the irregular bark on each tree, our right hemisphere grasps in one sweep the shape of the whole forest, relates it adroitly to the contours of the near landscape, then to the line of the horizon."

2. LH excels in verbal and symbolic processing of information; RH relies more on imagery than language. RH is superior in dealing with visual, tactile, or auditory stimuli that are hard to label or describe verbally and in handling spatial relationships.

3. LH is more interested in semantic similarity; RH is more interested in structural similarity.

4. LH processes information sequentially; RH processes it simultaneously.

5. LH works logically; RH works metaphorically and intuitively.

From this list it is obvious that both hemispheres are needed in research, where we must analyze information (primarily a LH process) and we must also synthesize it (a RH process). We must verbally process information (a LH activity) to record and report it. We must think intuitively "to see things that never were" and metaphorically to find new similarities—patterns or regularities (both RH processes). We must test our intuitions and metaphors for internal consistency and completeness and for consistency with other knowledge (a LH process). The primary process of imagery is more prominent in RH than LH processes.

Normally, both hemispheres are active and interact through the corpus callosum. But evidently the communication between them is incomplete because the RH can do things that the LH is unaware of. To quote Austin (1978, p. 139) again, "The right hemisphere . . . basically is *non*verbal. . . . Hidden away, almost out of reach of language [in the RH], [it] can be the source of intuitive insights that are of fundamental importance in solving a problem. And this hemisphere . . . is mute." It is as though the RH has intense need for personal privacy. It is willing to share its products, or at least some of them, with the conscious partner. But it refuses to share its secrets on the processes that lead to these products. It has deep secrets that it jealously keeps even from the proprietor of the body in which it resides.

Some people are LH dominant and others are RH dominant. Females may be less lateralized than males. Some people have hypothesized that the LH is the location of secondary processes and the RH is the location of primary processes, but some believe this to be unlikely.

What to do if you are like the person in the introductory paragraph who often "is of two minds" and your logical mind and intuitive mind provide different answers? The best choice, if you have enough time and money, is to reconcile them. If you lack the time and money and must act before you can reconcile them, keep score of right answers and select the answer provided by whichever hemisphere has been correct more often in the past.

5 *Too much innovation?*

HUTCHISON (1977, p. 57) has expressed a common view:

It is obvious that the difficulties of testing, or falsifying, are generally incomparably greater in economics than in physics. In the social sciences the ratio of conjectures to refutations (the plethora of conjectures and the paucity of refutations) is significantly higher. Theories and "programmes" in economics and the social sciences tend to have extremely long lives, surviving often in a stagnant or semi-moribund condition. . . . In fact, in the social sciences and economics, intellectual overpopulation is a chronic condition.

Lest I be charged with encouraging worse "intellectual overpopulation" of theories or models, remember that we also need imaginative and rigorous attacks on the methodological problems that Hutchison (1977) and Salmon (1973) raise and on numerous economic questions.

Salmon uses paradoxes to show that the logic of testing, confirming, and disconfirming hypotheses is not well understood. The raven paradox dramatically raises the issue of distinguishing between relevant and irrelevant confirmation. The hypothesis in this paradox is, "All ravens are black." This is logically equivalent to the statement, "All nonblack things are nonravens." Evidence that confirms this statement therefore confirms the hypothesis. Observation of a green vase (a nonblack thing that is a nonraven) confirms the hypothesis. "There seems to be something wrong" (Salmon 1973, p. 76). Salmon distinguishes "incremental" confirmation from "absolute" confirmation and demonstrates that, in the former, evidence that increases the probability of a proposition can decrease the probability of one of its consequences. He also shows how it is possible that an experimental result that confirms each of two hypotheses can reject the conjunction of the two hypotheses.

That the question raised by Salmon is relevant to economics is shown by McCloskey's (1983, pp. 495–99) description of economists' tests of the hypothesis of international purchasing power parity. He writes that half the economists conclude that the purchasing power parity hypothesis works and half conclude it does not.

Among the economic questions needing innovative study are these. To what extent should economists pattern their methodology after the physicists? What methods can economists adopt or adapt from the other social sciences to improve our ability to use survey data in hypothesis testing? What methods can we borrow from these disciplines that we can use to test assumptions about peoples' values, preferences, and desired public policy goals? Public policy choices have economic causes as well as economic consequences. What can we learn from the political scientists that will further our understanding of the process by which public policies are chosen? What are the possibilities of bringing economic analysis of public policy into closer alignment with reality by combining present welfare economics with measures of social indicators? On social indicators, see, for example, Fox (1974, 1983).

One can have considerable sympathy for Hutchison's complaint and yet value innovation. Responses to Hutchison were provided by Shubik (1970) and Hirshleifer (1985). Shubik predicted, and evidently approved of, developments that would join institutional detail, mathematical economic theory, and political economy and argues for more "special theories of limited scope, but with considerable application" (p. 407) that deal with different facets of the same economic problem because we pay too high a price to obtain general theory. Hirshleifer argued that "good economics will also have to be good anthropology and sociology and political science and psychology" (p. 53). In my career the lack of even one suitable model has been a problem much more often than has the existence of a superfluity of competing models.

6 Stages of scientific invention

WALLAS (1926, Ch. 4) has described the inventive process as consisting of four stages. Hughes (1963, pp. 97–101) has identified two other stages in the inventive process. The six stages are interest, preparation, incubation, illumination, verification, and exploitation.

Without interest the later steps will not follow. But interest by itself is not enough. You also need time, and the amount you will devote to a problem depends upon your priorities and prior commitments. Consequently, this step in the creative process can be described as development of a strong enough interest so that you will devote some of your scarce research resources to the question at hand. But interest itself has to be preceded by awareness. You must become aware of a problem to be solved, an anomaly to be explained, a contradiction to be resolved, a question to be asked before you can develop an interest.

Preparation is a conscious, voluntary, willful effort that is required to stimulate the subconscious. The rules for the preparation stage include "the whole traditional art of logic, the mathematical forms of which are the logic of the modern experimental sciences, and the methods of systematic and continuous examination of present or recorded phenomena . . . and the voluntary choice of a 'problem-attitude.' Our mind is not likely to give us a clear answer to any particular problem unless we set it a clear question. . ." (Wallas 1926, p. 84). Sometimes it is useful to perform mental experiments to investigate possible solutions. Identifying the adequacies and inadequacies of the solutions provides further understanding of the problem. Preparation is obviously an important step, but no more will be said about it here because problem formulation is a part of preparation and will be discussed at length in Section 11. Also, Section 21 on problem solving will have some things to say that are relevant to preparation.

The incubation stage is a stage of unconscious mental activity. "During incubation we do not voluntarily or consciously think on a particular problem and . . . a series of unconscious and involuntary . . . mental activities may take place" (Wallas 1926, p. 86). This stage calls for the exercise of patience. The conscious cannot will the unconscious mind to give birth to a bright idea on demand.

Illumination is the same as Beveridge's (1957) "sudden enlightenment or comprehension." The preparation and illumination stages imply some sort of communication between the conscious and the unconscious. In preparation, messages pass from the conscious to the unconscious; in illumination, messages move in the other direction.

Verification is also a conscious, voluntary, willful effort that is guided by the same rules as preparation. One purpose of verification is to express the results completely and precisely in language or writing. Deductive reasoning plays an important role here. All logical consequences of our theory must be deduced so that the theory can be fully tested. It is not sufficient, for example, to quit a retroductive argument as soon as you have explained the phenomena you wanted to account for. You must derive the other logical consequences of the assumptions and submit them to testing. A retroductive argument that satisfactorily explains some phenomena but contradicts other experience clearly is in need of further work. A theory that can do no more than explain something already observed has weaker support than a theory that can also correctly predict things that have not been observed.

Another purpose of verification is to test the illumination: to test it against logic or mathematical rules, experience, and other knowledge. A third purpose of verification is to prepare for using the illumination. We see that this step involves more than Popper's (1959, pp. 32–33) four tests of a theory. It involves the prior (to testing) steps of obtaining a complete and precise expression and the subsequent step of preparing one's self to exploit the invention. In place of the more accurate expression "completion, clarification, testing, and preparation for use", I will use Wallas's "verification," with apologies to followers of Popper for the discomfort I cause them.

The last step is exploitation. Without it, the preceding steps will have negligible impact.

Typically, a person is simultaneously engaged in two or more of these stages on two or more problems. Conscious verification of one answer serves as preparation for unconscious effort on a second question while the unconscious is incubating on a third. In practice, work on any single problem usually does not follow these steps in strict sequence. Rather, an investigator jumps back and forth from one step to another. Perhaps verification shows that the proposed solution is inadequate and you then return to preparation to identify the nature of the inadequacy and follow this by incubation and another illumination. The completed product is almost always the result of several intuitions or hunches. The process of verifying also serves as preparation for the next step in the creative process. The quotation from Weld in Section 3 covers the first five stages. The psychologist Hutchinson (1949) has perceptively found another stage: the stage of frustration, which comes after preparation. It seems more accurate to me to label frustration, not as a stage, but as an emotion that one is likely to experience at any time (probably several times) during the process of invention.

PART II

Conditions stimulating to unconscious mental processes

UNCONSCIOUS MINDS do respond to stimuli, but not all respond to the same ones; minds that do respond to the same stimuli do not all do so in the same degree. My reading, discussions, and introspection lead me to believe that many people's unconscious minds do respond to the conditions discussed here.

 7 *Doubt*

IF YOU ARE convinced that we have adequate procedures for measuring price elasticities of consumer demand, you will not develop a better method. If you believe that existing theory of cooperative behavior is adequate, you will not develop a better theory. If you believe that all existing theories, models, and measures are adequate, you will not develop anything better. If you believe all significant questions have been properly asked, you will never ask a new important question. If you do not doubt something, you will have nothing to research; if you doubt nothing, you are not justified in doing research because you are doing unneeded work. Some people doubt only what they have been taught to doubt. It can prove fruitful to doubt what no one else has doubted. You will never solve a problem that you are unaware of. "Necessity is the mother of invention" is an old saying. My reading of history leads me to believe that dissatisfaction also has been the mother of many inventions.

I am not suggesting here that you go through life doubting everything. I am only claiming that in those instances when you are most dissatisfied with accepted modes of thought or conventional questions or approaches your unconscious is more likely to generate new ideas.

It may make it easier for you to doubt and to venture if you will realize that our assumptions are only that and not statements of fact. Our arguments run, "If businesses maximize profits, then Y," or, "If consumers maximize this sort of function, then Z." In the minds of some, including, unfortunately, many professors, the conditional if has been translated into because.

Prince's statement (1970, p. 78), "As the expert accumulates the specific knowledge that makes him so valuable he also incorporates accepted certainties that are not really certain," expresses the truth that not all the experts' certainties will bear up under careful scrutiny. Some of our basic assumptions have reasonable alternatives that have not been thoroughly investigated.

It is not enough merely to doubt. It is necessary to resolve the doubts, to venture answers.

8   *Venturesome attitude*

YOU ARE NOT going to break new ground by developing a new model or theory or measure by asking a new question if you are paralyzed by the fear of making a mistake. Do not be afraid to make mistakes! There are plenty of people around who will delight in pointing out your errors. Think how much pleasure you will afford those people if you do make a mistake. I think it was John Maynard Keynes who astutely observed, "It is not so terrible to make a mistake. What is terrible is not to be found out." After all, by the time each of us finishes formal schooling, we have been caught in enough mistakes that we know that being found out does not destroy our ego, self-esteem, or self-worth. Being caught in a mistake after leaving school is no more destructive of your self-esteem than being caught while still in school.

It is probably not so much fear of making mistakes that inhibits us as it is fear of failure. If a failure now and then is going to ruin your career or your self-esteem, your successes must not be worth much. Perhaps this suggests a career that is a mixture of some safe and some risky projects so that your successes on the safe projects can compensate for possible failures on the risky ones.

We can also infer the desirability of having both risky and safe projects from Schultz's (1982, p. 189) writings on research entrepreneurship: "The very essence of research is the fact that it is a dynamic venture into the unknown or into what is only partially known. Research . . . is inescapably subject to risk and uncertainty. . . . An important factor in producing knowledge is the human ability I shall define as *research entrepreneurship*." Economists believe that entrepreneurship is important to a dynamic economy. Schultz argues that we scientists should also value research entrepreneurship. Presumably then we can relate each researcher's portfolio of safe and risky projects to his or her degree of risk aversion or risk affection.

Schultz's insight reflects sound psychology. Torrance (1962, pp. 72–76, Ch. 6) believes that creative people are "prudent risk-takers" who "test the limits very carefully and cautiously and withdraw with the greatest of speed from a dangerous situation" (p. 74). They are, like astronauts, risk takers but not reckless. They prepare for testing the limits.

We may also wonder if a researcher who fails to venture into the unknown, who selects only safe projects, is providing an employer a fair return for the money. "Mediocre results are no adequate return for the employment of high gifts, and may not even repay the money spent on achieving them" (Polanyi 1958, p. 124).

If you have a mixture of safe and risky projects, you will soon learn that failure, like success, is unpredictable. On some projects I have failed to achieve what I thought were modest objectives that I believed I knew how to attain when I began work. In other cases I have achieved objectives that I had absolutely no idea how to accomplish when I initiated a project.

One reason for this may be some sort of compensatory principle. A greater curiosity about, interest in, or challenge by the risky project may have elicited more thorough preparation and more effort. As will be seen in later sections, interest, curiosity, challenge, preparation, and effort all serve to stimulate mental processes. Too, a magnificent failure can be more exciting than a modest success. One thing is certain, few things in life are more gratifying than accomplishing a task that one believed to be impossible. It is appropriate here to recall what Pogo (in Walt Kelly's comic strip of the same name) once observed, "We are confronted with insurmountable opportunities."

We need to understand clearly whether it is making mistakes or whether it is criticism for making mistakes that we fear. The distinction is meaningful because it is not true that the best way to avoid criticism for our mistakes is to make none. No indeed! The best way to avoid criticism for our mistakes is to make the same ones everyone else makes.

Some people suffer from an exaggerated fear of failure because they have an exaggerated view of success. They have a polar view of creative results: a view that a creative effort produces a grand, majestic product worthy of a Pulitzer or Nobel Prize, or at least a fellowship in a professional association, or else it is a failure. This view is blatantly false. Most successful efforts at creativity result in modest successes.

But even modest successes give the inventor a satisfaction that can come only from invention and never comes from imitation, and they do contribute to our knowledge.

Burke (1978, p. 288) wrote:

In the heroic treatment [of history,] historical change is shown to have been generated by the genius of individuals, conveniently labelled "inventors." In such a treatment, Edison invented the electric light, Bell the telephone, Gutenberg the printing press, Watt the steam engine, and so on. But no individual is responsible for producing an invention *ex nihilo*. The elevation of the single inventor to the position of sole creator at best exaggerates his influence over events, and at worst denies the involvement of those humbler members of society without whose work his task might have been impossible.

Even in those cases where the single inventor would have succeeded without the contributions of the "humbler members of society," the task would have been more difficult and the invention delayed without their contributions.

Some people have an exaggerated fear of failure because they overestimate the intelligence needed for creativity. The relation between creative ability and intelligence has been much studied, and the following conclusion seems firmly established. Among people who have enough intelligence to receive a graduate degree, intelligence and creative ability are independently distributed. Another point that most psychologists accept is that IQ is an inadequate measure of intelligence and that cognitive abilities exist that are not recognized in IQ tests.

The creation of something new requires some departure from an established system. The very familiarity and general acceptance of an established system make it easy to be comfortable within it. You generally can limit your risk by staying within that system. To break away from it is to plunge into the unknown, which can be scary. This plunge can result in failure to find something new and can be harmful to your career if you stay outside the established system too long without success. But a plunge into the unknown can also be exhilarating. And is not the opportunity to probe the unknown one of the features of science that causes people to become scientists? If you are perceptive, you cannot always be satisfied with the established order in your discipline. You recognize that you must either ignore some important problems or handle them inadequately, or you must step into the unknown to create a new piece of knowledge that is more adequate than what you now have.

The social psychologist Aronson reminds us that errors can be productive and that mistakes can be useful (1981, pp. 5–6):

> Science is a self-corrective enterprise. . . . if I do a study that *isn't* perfect, it will soon be improved upon by others. Thus, my goal is to get it into the literature to give my colleagues a chance to look at it, be stimulated by it, be provoked by it, annoyed by it, and then go ahead and do it better even if their intent is to prove me wrong and even if they succeed in proving me wrong. . . . I have faith that if I do an imperfect piece of work, someone will read it and will be provoked to demonstrate this imperfection in a really interesting way. This will almost always lead to a greater understanding of the phenomenon under investigation. . . .
>
> Since I believe that science is a self-correcting enterprise, I would prefer to be provocative than right. . . .
>
> As I read the journals, it seems to me that a lot of the fun has gone out of social psychology. One of the reasons for this, I think, is that we've gotten much too cautious, much too careful, much too afraid to be wrong, and it's taken a lot of the zest and a lot of the yeast out of the research in social psychology.

One thrust of this quotation seems to be that we have forgotten the functions of professional journals. Individually, we concentrate upon the value of journal articles as self-promotional tools and neglect their importance as a means for the development of our discipline.

Virtually all present knowledge originated as a hunch in some individual's mind. If these individuals had not dared to speculate, to dream, we would have no more science, art, and religion than our pet cats have. We have today's knowledge only because individuals have dared to venture into the unknown. And the need to explore the unknown is no less than in the past. Our ignorance is greater now than ever before. As the volume of our sphere of knowledge grows, the area of its surface of ignorance also grows.

It may be true that every single thing you know is known better by some of your colleagues. But a career is not built from single bits of knowledge; it is built of combinations. You may be able to form useful combinations that none of your colleagues can. If it is useful, it does not even need to be a combination that no colleague can form. It is enough if few colleagues have formed it.

You should recognize that your successful colleagues do not look nearly as clever, smart, or brilliant to themselves as they look to you.

You know their successes, but they know their failures. Their successes are reported in books, journal articles, seminars. Their failures end up in their wastebaskets. Sometimes even their successes do not look nearly as good to them as they do to you because they know how much more they had hoped to accomplish than they did. They know the agony and frustration and false starts that went into these beautiful studies, which they could have completed more quickly if they had been smarter; you see only the beautiful analysis. One reason your successful colleagues look better to you than to themselves was presented previously: research reports do not tell how research is done.

Some scientists are more successful than others in spite of having had more failures. They have had more bad ideas but also more good ideas. And they have been able to discriminate.

A willingness to tackle the unknown requires some self-confidence. But, my goodness, by the time you are a graduate student, you have already successfully tackled the unknown many times. When you were an eighth grader, high school was an unknown; when you were a twelfth grader, college was an unknown; when you were a senior, graduate school was an unknown. You should have developed some self-confidence from having met those earlier challenges successfully. That "one cannot know what he is capable of unless he tests his limits" (Torrance 1962, p. 74) is still true even if you have a Ph.D. There is no good reason to stop testing your limits just because you are no longer taking courses. If you have never failed, you have never reached your limits, and probably have never done the best work you are capable of doing.

It can even be profitable to assume impossible things or ask impossible questions. Doing so can lead to valuable insights that will not come from possible assumptions or questions. This is allied to two practices of the synectics group approach to problem solving (Prince 1970): (1) pushing a basic law or concept to its limit and (2) "force-fitting." In force-fitting, a problem and a strange or impossible solution are forced to fit together by redefining, stretching, twisting, or anything else that can be done to them to make them fit. One example is the get-fired solution in which the group considers a solution that is so outlandish it would get anyone fired who proposed it. This challenges the imagination to make the solution palatable, perhaps by a combination of modifying the solution and finding strong arguments that make it acceptable.

Some writers have observed that creative people are a restless breed. The restlessness perhaps springs from a discontent, a divine dissatisfaction, with the current state of knowledge.

A notable result that Torrance (1962, p. 78) and others obtained in studies of creativity in children is that the highly creative children's work "is characterized by humor, playfulness, relative lack of rigidity, and relaxation." This playful attitude seems to stay with productive researchers. See Wallach and Kogan (1965). I have often heard such people speak of playing around with some ideas or having great fun with a research project. In talking about the period when he did the work that earned him the Nobel Prize, the physicist Feynman stated (1983, pp. 7–8):

And somehow or other I could relax about this and I thought to myself, "I haven't done anything important, and I'm never going to do anything important, but I used to enjoy physics and mathematical things. And because I used to play with it, it was never very important, but I used to do things for the fun of it." So I decided I'm going to do things only for the fun of it. . . . I relaxed and started to play, played as I said with this rotation. And this rotation led me to a problem — a similar problem of the rotation of the spin of an electron, according to Dirac's equation. And that just led me back into quantum electrodynamics, which is the problem I'd been working on. And I kept continuing now to play with it in the relaxed fashion I had originally done. And everything — it was just like taking the cork out of a bottle — everything just poured out. I, by the way, in very short order worked the things out for which I later won the Nobel Prize.

This may be the oddest bisociation of all: that successful scientists take their discipline seriously but approach it with a playful attitude. Let it be noted, however, that they do not approach it frivolously.

Galbraith (1960, pp. 1–2) has suggested one explanation of this paradox. He writes that solemnity "is a serious source of inflexibility. Change and new evidence have a way of making previous convictions seem odd, even ridiculous. The reasonably relaxed man can accept correction without too grievous loss of dignity. But the solemn man cannot. He may have heard that the truth will set him free. But he rightly senses that it might also make him seem silly." Successful scientists recognize that the search for truth is too important to be treated solemnly.

A more fundamental explanation is that this is not really a paradox. Much of the play of young humans, and of young mammals in general, is an exploration, a search, a hunt. The search is part of the fun. Also, puzzle solving is one form of play. And scientists are puzzle solvers. Finally, I suspect that the relaxed, playful attitude is closely connected to the willingness to use unconscious mental processes. It is also significant that science and play both make use of models. Playing children use model people (dolls), playhouses, and play furniture; toy cars, trucks, and horses are among their models; they construct model airplanes, model cars, and model boats. They use these toys to create their own worlds. Scientists also create their own worlds when they create models. Huizinga (1950) has probably seen as clearly as anyone the similarities between play and science: "Into an imperfect world and into the confusion of life, [play] brings a temporary, a limited perfection. Play demands order absolute and supreme"(p. 10). And, "All play has its rules" (p. 11). Also, "Play can very well include seriousness" (p. 45).

The analogy between research and play can easily mislead us. Participation in a game is not inconsistent with discipline, dedication, serious thought, goal orientation, and hard work. To convince ourselves of this, we need only look at participants in the Olympic Games. All athletes who become the best that they can be combine these drives with their innate physical talents. Scientists who become the best that they can be also bring these drives to their research. Very few people, Olympians or otherwise, play games to lose. Part of the apparent paradox arises from a fundamental ambiguity in the words "work" and "play." The difference between work and play is not in one's activity, but in one's attitude. When my neighbor and I are simultaneously mowing our lawns, I am engaged in yard "work" and he in yard "play" because I dislike the activity and he enjoys it. Fly-fishing is play, but I will happily expend more physical and mental effort on it than on yard work.

Lest this and the preceding section seem to demand too much from a person, it is perhaps appropriate to end with a quotation from Taylor (1963, p. 366). He begins with a reference to Anne Roe, a well-known student of creativity:

In a discussion with Anne Roe, I received the impression that many of her eminent scientists needed only to have two or three high-quality ideas for development each year in order to add other good links to their usually continuous chain of research studies. To maintain sustained production in science, a scientist may need only one new good idea to pursue within a reasonable period of time after he finishes a previous piece of work.

9 *Tolerance for uncertainty*

A NEW INSIGHT may contradict the accepted view of things. If the insight is intuitively compelling, you must live with the uncertainty of knowing contradictory things (the accepted view and the new insight) until you can reconcile them. And the reconciliation may take months. The emotions that you can experience during those months are humorously but accurately described by the jingle that Einstein wrote in a young admirer's autograph book: "A thought that sometimes makes me hazy/Am I or are the others crazy?" You can even have contradictory reactions to your own invention: "This must be wrong. It is so simple that many others must have already discovered it. The fact that it has not been published must mean that it's wrong." But, "Where is it wrong? I can't find a flaw in it. It must not be wrong." And then, "Maybe it's right. But it has not been published because it's not useful." However, "I can already see a number of applications. Aren't these applications important? On which days am I crazy? The days when I believe my idea's a good one? Or the days when I believe it's a bad one?" Months may pass before you finally decide whether your invention is right or wrong, useful or useless.

In the interim you must live with the question, Am I or are the others crazy? You can look at it this way: the uncertainty is a price that you pay for the chance to devise something new and valuable and exciting. If you find it unsettling to go for an extended period without knowing the answer to Einstein's question, you will find an inventive career to be decidedly uncomfortable.

New insights are often vague, incomplete, or fragmentary. A long time may elapse before you are certain that you can produce a useful product from them. In the interim you must live with the uncertainty of not knowing whether the ideas that you have are any good. Also, because of these three characteristics of new insights, it follows that an ability to suspend judgment is a necessary attribute for successful research. A new insight, no matter its potential, has little chance of being accepted if you judge it before it is completed or before you thoroughly understand it. Parnes (1966, pp. 241–47) summarizes research on the principle of deferred judgment, which "calls for deliberate deferment of judgment during idea-finding in order to prevent premature judgment from hampering imagination, judgment being applied *after* a wide variety of alternatives is listed."

The research shows that both individuals and groups produce more good ideas when using deferred judgment than when using concurrent evaluation of ideas. Arieti (1976, pp. 376–77) also writes of the desirability of separating our creative thinking periods from our critical thinking periods. We should not allow our conscious, critical thought processes to intrude on our times of unconscious creative thinking.

Every scientist, whether inventive or not, must have a high tolerance for uncertainty because our knowledge is tentative. We cannot know what the world is like. At most, we can know what we now think the world is like. And frequently we are confused about that. Three of our tools for understanding the world are economic theory, statistical theory, and data. Economic theory is an abstraction, an approximation of reality. Statistical theory is also only an approximate description of the processes that generate our data and provides only probabilistic results. Our data contain errors of measurement, and some of our measured variables are only proxy variables. When I contemplate all the possible sources of error in our present knowledge, the possibility that a new development will contain error causes me little discomfort. After all, one infinity of possible errors is no larger than another.

You cannot have a high tolerance for uncertainty unless you also have a large capacity to recognize and admit your own errors. In Section 8 I quoted Galbraith on solemnity. This quotation leads me to hypothesize that solemnity and high tolerance for uncertainty are mutually incompatible, and solemnity and venturesome attitude are also. Solemn people fear that making a mistake or admitting error makes them look silly. I also suspect that there is a close psychological connection between an ability to admit error and taking a playful approach to serious research. It is consistent with a playful approach to accept the fact that you will make mistakes. Accepting this makes it easier to relax your conscious controls and inhibitions and let your unconscious roam at will. You know that a mistake is not a fatality, it is merely something to be corrected.

It is a mistake to believe that you cannot be fully committed to research unless you are completely satisfied with the available research methods. You can properly use a research method, feeling secure in the knowledge that it is the best available while simultaneously being unhappy that it is not as good a method as you would like to have. Doubt and uncertainty need not preclude commitment.

✺ 10 Diversity

A FRUITFUL INTUITION is often the perception of a connection between things that were previously unconnected. It then follows that one condition favorable to a fruitful unconscious is diversity of memories, experiences, and interests. Young (1951, p. 70) argues that those people who continue learning new things longer than others probably do so because they "constantly seek new circumstances." From his studies of problem solving, the psychologist Raaheim (1974, p. 87) has concluded that "the more experienced you are, the more problems you are likely to be faced with. And, to diminish a possible feeling of contradiction here, the more problems you are likely to solve." Our later discussion of problem solving (Section 21) will justify his statement. Many other writers have discussed the importance of diversity as a stimulus to unconscious mental activity. Among them are Hadamard (1954), Porterfield (1941), and Austin (1978). The diversity of interests and experiences need not all be professional. Austin, for example, emphasizes that research results are the accomplishments of the whole person, not just of a compartmentalized "professional" portion of a person. Avocations can contribute to one's vocation. Austin shows how his hobbies of music, watercolor painting, and hunting have influenced his research in neurology. It is reported that Einstein commented that the Russian novelist Dostoevsky "gave me more than any thinker, more than Gauss" (Kuznetsov 1979, p. 178).

A person can acquire diverse experiences vicariously by reading on a wide variety of topics. Mighell (1976, p. 120) has recommended "offbeat reading." "Much of it may not seem to have any practical application, but it is the kind that results in the mind stretching, wrenching, and jolting that fires the imagination and brings forth new ideas. It is that which opens up new avenues and sends thought beyond the usual horizon." Three fictional works that Mighell found helpful to him are Poe's "The Purloined Letter," Wilder's *The Bridge of San Luis Rey*, and Bellamy's *Looking Backward*. The discussion of the unconscious and bisociations in science in Section 3 mentioned the key role that reading Malthus's *Essay* played in Darwin's development of the theory of evolution. Darwin said that he read the *Essay* "for amusement."

Keynes certainly believed that an economist must know more than economics. In his biography of Alfred Marshall he wrote (1963, p. 141):

The master-economist must possess a rare *combination* of gifts. He must reach a high standard in several different directions and must combine talents not often found together. He must be mathematician, historian, statesman, philosopher — in some degree. He must understand symbols and speak in words. He must contemplate the particular in terms of the general, and touch abstract and concrete in the same flight of thought. He must study the present in the light of the past for the purposes of the future. No part of man's nature or his institutions must lie entirely outside his regard. He must be purposeful and disinterested in a simultaneous mood; as aloof and incorruptible as an artist, yet sometimes as near the earth as a politician. Much, but not all, of this ideal many-sidedness Marshall possessed.

That Keynes himself was a many-sided person whose knowledge and interest encompassed many things besides economics is evidenced by his *Essays in Biography* and by Heilbroner's (1983) character sketch of him.

Myrdal (1958, p. 40) was successively university economics professor, government adviser, parliament member, student of the American Negro problem, cabinet minister, central bank director, and international civil servant. He wrote from this broad perspective:

The demand for the highest expertness in scientific work must always be preserved; but I see no reason why a social scientist should be tied to only one specialty and for his whole life. There has been, and is, much intellectual inbreeding in our traditional academic disciplines. The confrontation with practical tasks, the cooperation with scientists from other disciplines, and the constant transgressions of the old boundary lines will feed us all with new ideas, make us relate the part to the whole, and fructify scientific thought over the entire world.

Evsey Domar's career is evidence of the value of diversity to an economist. He was named 1984 Distinguished Fellow of the American Economic Association. The last sentence in his fellowship citation read (Am. Econ. Assoc. 1985, p. 289), "As a student of the economy of the USSR, as an analyst of the cooperative firm, and as a propounder of an extraordinarily fruitful historical generalization about the origin of slave and serf systems, his example has taught a generation of economists the value of a broad historical, geographical, and institutional imagination."

The statistician R. A. Fisher was strongly interested in genetics. His development of factorial block experimental designs grew from his understanding of Mendelian genetics and his observation of a close parallel between genetic and experimental situations. See Box (1980) for details. I can recall various times when my economic research benefited from cross-fertilization by other disciplines:

1. My undergraduate courses in psychology helped me write my Ph.D. dissertation in econometric method.

2. Knowledge of a psychometric method, factor analysis, provided a clue to development of a model of prices and demands for product characteristics.

3. Work with animal breeders stimulated my work on microeconomics of technical change.

4. A variant of my work on technical change led to development of a method for measuring value of information.

5. Study of group dynamics and labor economics furthered my understanding of agricultural cooperatives, and study of cooperatives in turn enabled me to construct a model of an agricultural labor union.

6. Some of my deepest insights into the nature of economics have not come from studying economics; they have come from studying economists.

In his study of creativity, the psychiatrist Arieti coined the term "creativogenic" to describe cultures or societies that promote creativity. He discussed (1976, pp. 312–25) nine characteristics of a creativogenic society. Of these nine, no less than five favor opportunities for diverse personal experiences and influences: (1) availability of cultural means, (2) openness to cultural stimuli, (3) free access to cultural media for all citizens without discrimination, (4) exposure to different and even contrasting cultural stimuli, and (5) interaction of significant persons.

A varied store of memories and experiences is a benefit and a challenge. It is a benefit because it makes it possible for the unconscious to perceive connections between things that one would not even be aware of if one's experiences were less varied. It is also a challenge because it increases the number of things one knows without realizing it. One of the advantages an experienced investigator has over a young researcher is that the former has a more varied store of memories and experiences upon which to draw. Diversity not only helps you find solutions to present problems, it helps you identify problems whose solutions you know. And it can introduce you to exciting new problems.

A new connection between unlike things that leads to a discovery need not be part of the discovered product. The connection may exist only in the discoverer's mind and never be made public: another reason why a report of research results is not a report of research process. If the link provides a new insight or solution, it has served a useful purpose even though it is never perceived by anyone else or publicized by the discoverer.

It is not enough merely to know diverse things; you must also know each thing in diverse ways. Some psychologists' findings on learning, retention, and memory are worth discussing here. Psychologists agree that meaningfulness facilitates learning. An item's meaningfulness is measured by the number of things you associate with it. If you associate many things with an item, you know it in many ways. If you associate diverse things with it, you know it in diverse ways.

Also important is the relation of meaning to memory, that is, to retention and recall. The stronger the original learning of something, the longer it is retained. Being able to associate some new fragment of knowledge with many other prior pieces strengthens the learning of the new and increases its retention time. Making an association between a new bit of knowledge and a previous bit also increases the retention time of the previous knowledge. But it is not sufficient simply to retain material in long-term memory; the material must also be retrievable. The degree to which something is retrievable depends on the ability to form associations and networks of associations among items in the memory. Your future ability to retrieve something learned today depends upon your ability to construct mental associations among items already in the memory and items learned today. It also depends on your ability to construct associations among items learned today and items learned in the future. Knowing something in many and diverse ways makes it more easily retrievable because it is associated with many and diverse other items in the memory.

Consider three items A, B, and C in the memory with B connected to A and to C as in Figure 10.1. Various ways in which A may be retrieved from memory are:

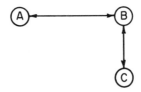

10.1. Three items in the memory.

1. Retrieve A directly.
2. Retrieve B and its association with something other than C. Reconstruct or reinvent A.
3. Retrieve B. Reconstruct or reinvent its association with something other than C. Reconstruct or reinvent A.
4. Retrieve C. Reconstruct or reinvent its association with B and reconstruct or reinvent B. Then do as in step 3.
5. Retrieve C and its association with something other than A. Reconstruct or reinvent B. Then do as in step 3.
6. Retrieve C. Reconstruct or reinvent its association with something other than A. Reconstruct or reinvent B. Then retrieve B's association with A and reconstruct or reinvent A.

This list is probably not exhaustive, but it is sufficient to make the point. If either C or its association with B is not in the memory, the last three procedures are not available. If only A is in the memory, or if its association with B is not in the memory, then only the first procedure (direct recall) is available.

In this example, the associations are among unitary percepts or items. Associations may also be among networks of associations. Many of the associative elements that we use in research are relations such as implication, sufficiency, equivalence, transitivity, greater than, preferred to, and so forth, and chains of such relationships. Let a known relation between A and B be expressed as ARB. This may not be the same as BRA. Use of relationships is a way of expressing and also of organizing our knowledge. Gestalt psychologists view *coherence* of elements A and B as resulting from the fusion of unitary percepts A and B and knowledge of R into the single new item ARB in the memory. Such organization facilitates learning and memory. As one writer expressed it, "Connect, connect, always connect." Make connections among different disciplines and different experiences. For example, use your knowledge of psychology to enhance your understanding of economics and vice versa.

In discussing the role of these conscious connections in aiding recall, psychologists write of "retrieval cues" (that must be established during learning or relearning and lead to recall of the cued items), "interitem dependencies," "associative chains and networks," and "unitizing" and "chunking" (which mean increasing the amount of information in each unit recalled). See Tulving and Donaldson (1972).

It may be helpful to present an example of knowing in diverse ways and of associations. Linear programming provides a useful illustrative vehicle because it is a familiar topic to most economists. The specific parts of a linear program that will be discussed are shadow prices or criterion elements of a maximization problem. Among the things that can be known about shadow prices are (1) mathematical derivation; (2) methods of computation; (3) role in simplex method; (4) economic interpretation in familiar problems; (5) how to derive their interpretation in unfamiliar problems; (6) their relation to the solution to the dual; (7) their use in sensitivity analysis; (8) how they can be used to study effects of certain kinds of technological change; and (9) their use in studying economics of product quality, grades, and standards.

One type of knowing in diverse ways involves understanding the derivation of a proposition, its general implications, and its specific interpretations in different applications. For example, item 4 in the preceding list is a specific application of the general procedure in 5, item 7 is an application of 6, and items 8 and 9 are specific applications of the general concept in 7.

It is desirable to be able to grasp the general idea that lies behind a specific idea because the general can be more easily transposed or transferred than can the specific. Consider, for example, a student who has been taught theory of a profit-maximizing competitive firm, who has studied first- and second-order conditions for determining quantities of inputs and outputs that maximize profit, who has been shown how the second-order conditions and the bordered Hessian condition are used to determine the effect of variation in an input or output price upon the profit-maximizing levels of inputs and outputs, and who can apply all these operations to a numerical problem in an examination. What if this same student cannot answer the question, Suppose that a parameter in the production function of this firm changes so that each combination of inputs results in a larger level of outputs. What is the effect of this change upon the firm's profit? One explanation is that the student understands the specific but not the general that lies behind it. A student who understood the specific problem taught in class and the general concept behind it would comprehend several things:

1. Determining the effect of a variation in price upon quantities of inputs and outputs involves determining the effect of a change in a parameter upon the quantity variables.

2. Changing a coefficient in the production function is a change in a parameter of the problem, as is a change in price.

3. The same sort of mathematical argument used to study effect of variation in one parameter upon quantities can be used to study effect of variation in another parameter upon these same quantities.

4. Because prices are assumed fixed in this second problem, after effects of a change in the production function are known, the effect upon profit is determinate.

Being able to grasp the general that lies behind the specific means, for example, realizing that determining the effect of variation in price received upon level of output of a profit-maximizing firm is a specific instance of determining the effect of a change in one of the parameters of an optimization problem upon the values of the instrument variables and upon the value of the objective function.

Finally, it is not enough to know diverse things in diverse ways and to be able to recall them. It is also necessary that you be willing to use any of them on any problem. If you have not yet solved a problem, you cannot know which matrices should be bisociated to provide a solution. And if you do not know this, you cannot know which matrices are irrelevant to your problem. If someone else has solved a problem, it is still possible that you know a combination of matrices that person did not know and that can be bisociated to form a better solution. Remember, we are all ignorant. We are just ignorant about different things.

It is not enough to be able to apply a method of analysis to the problems that your professors have taught you to apply it to. Life does not restrict itself to asking of you only the questions that your professors ask. Actually, life does not ask you any questions at all. It is up to you as a scientist to ask the questions.

Indirect evidence on the value of diversity comes from studying the backgrounds of many inventors. In his history of inventions de Bono (1974, p. 9) wrote:

What was the famous astronomer Edmund Halley doing sitting under 60 ft. of water for an hour and a half? He was trying out his own invention, the diving bell. . . . It is not extraordinary to find an astronomer inventing a diving bell, for the history of inventions is full of examples of people who invented things outside their own fields. The first corn-reaper, for example, was produced by an actor, who demonstrated it on a crop he had "planted" on stage. The first practical submarine was invented by an Irish schoolmaster in New York, with the intention of sinking the British Navy. The pneumatic tyre was invented by a Scots vet called Dunlop to help his son ride his tricycle to school over rough cobblestones. The hydrofoil was first thought of by a French priest, and the knitting frame by an English vicar who failed to convince Queen Elizabeth I of its potential. The principles of flying were worked out by a Yorkshire squire who sent his unwilling coachman aloft in a glider, while the safety razor was invented by a 40-year-old salesman who was advised to invent something which would be used once and then thrown away — as we would say today, something disposable.

Arguments on the value of diversity turn out to be implicit attacks on much of our scientific education. As our knowledge of a discipline grows, we have more to teach students in each specialty. And the pressure grows to make each student's education narrower and deeper: to cut down on electives in order to impart the growing core of the discipline. Granted, we want our graduate schools to turn out experts. But I fear that it is becoming increasingly true that our graduates satisfy the pathological definition of expert: An expert is someone who has learned more and more about less and less until he knows everything there is to know about nothing. We could counteract this unfortunate trend if we followed Johnson's (1971) and Mosher's (1973) recommendation that every social science graduate student be required to participate in multidisciplinary exploration of selected problems.

I frequently think that economists have made a serious mistake in recent years by looking to other economists (and to mathematicians) as the sole source of useful knowledge. By claiming our discipline as the sole repository of social science wisdom and virtue, we have cut ourselves off from a number of useful developments in sociology, psychology, and political science. Our extreme professional egocentrism has fooled our new Ph.D. recipients into thinking that because they know economics they know what the world is like. They see theories and models of the world as being the real world and fail to see that they are merely devices for understanding the world. This narrowness has had some deplorable consequences. For example, some economists have applied their economics to animal breeding to help the animal breeders to become more efficient or to evaluate their efficiency, without bothering to learn even the simplest basic things about genetics or animal breeding. As a consequence, even though their economics was good, they have studied a world that animal breeders cannot recognize and have obtained results that have no relevance to animal breeding.

Variety in experience does not come simply from living. One must make a conscious effort to obtain it. A young assistant professor had failed to make this conscious effort. He had been at one school for three years when he learned of an open position at a university in California. He had long wanted to live in California, so he quickly applied for the position. In his application, he emphasized the benefit of his three years of experience. His department head, however, saw it differently. In his letter of reference he wrote, "This young man has not had three years of experience. He has had one year of experience three times." The story illustrates a danger that we need to guard against as we grow older in our profession. We must not confuse habit with experience.

11   *Thorough preparation*

THE WALLAS-HUGHES LIST of six stages of the inventive process (Section 6) labeled the second stage "preparation." The preparation stage precedes unconscious mental activity. The more thoroughly the conscious mind has grasped the problem (in general outline and in detail), the better is the chance that the unconscious will produce fruitful ideas. Unconscious processes are stimulated by vigorous conscious processes. How does one go about preparing thoroughly? The degree of thoroughness of your preparation is a function of your entire previous life history. The skills in observation, experimentation, perception, and discrimination and the knowledge of techniques that you currently bring to bear upon a problem have been developing through an entire lifetime. But what can you do now to prepare yourself to tackle the present problem? Pretend that we are applied economists who have had a problem brought to us by our employer and our job is to provide information that can be used to find a good solution.

This is only one possible situation. I choose it as the basis for discussion because it is probably the most restrictive. In this situation we are not free to formulate the problem as we would like it to be or to impose assumptions of convenience; we must formulate it in such a way that we will provide information that is useful to the employer. Nor can we formulate it so that we know that we can solve it. The result is likely to be a mess that is completely lacking in elegance and generality. As a rule, however, clients do not live in elegant, general worlds. Putting the discussion in this context does not limit its applicability as much as it might appear. Even the academic economists, whose contact with business people or public decision makers is limited to reading about them in newspapers and reading what other economists write about them in professional journals, usually claim that their results are useful for something or to somebody. Apparently they have in mind, at least implicitly, some possible users. Certainly,

when preparing research proposals to solicit financial support, economists do not hesitate to claim that their results will be useful to certain
people for solving their problems. I also believe that the person whose
motive is pure intellectual curiosity will find this discussion helpful.
More on this issue at the end of the section.

One step in thorough preparation for tackling the employer's
problem is for us to develop a proper formulation of it. Our employer
perceives and describes the problem in one language: nontechnical,
business and laypeople's. We must translate it into technical jargon
because that is what we use for formulating and investigating problems. Problem formulation was the first step we had to go through to
solve word problems in eighth-grade algebra, that is, to translate the
words into algebraic expressions.

The first task encountered in any research is formulating the
problem to be researched. Webster's dictionary defines formulate as to
put into a systematized statement or expression. So problem formulation means developing a systematized statement or expression of a
problem. Ferber and Verdoorn (1962, pp. 31–32) write that problem
formulation "helps to overcome much of the researcher's initial confusion by establishing a closer connection between the problem at hand
and the techniques that might be used in its solution." Problem formulation is likely to place greater demands on your ingenuity and
knowledge than will the subsequent process of investigating possible
solutions. Problem formulation is a creative process: creation of a
bridge between theory, models, or methods on the one hand and the
real world on the other. There are no recipes or rules that are guaran-
teed to provide this bridge; that is, there is no theory that tells us how
to apply theory. But systematic consideration of the questions presented here will help in formulating the problem our employer has
brought to us.

In his book *How to Solve It* (1957) Polya suggests and analyzes
methods for problem solving. His discussion is largely couched in
terms of solving a problem that has already been defined. The principles he presents, however, are applicable to the defining of a problem.
In large part, the discussion here is based on Polya's list of questions.

Where do answers to these questions come from? From the decision makers with or for whom the researcher is working. And people
who have worked with or studied the decision makers and their problems are obvious possibilities.

Quantitative economic policy. Before discussing the questions, elements of theory of quantitative economic policy will be summarized. The questions will make frequent use of the terminology of theory of quantitative economic policy. Elements of a flexible target model are:

1. The policymaker's welfare, objective, or utility function.
2. Target variables, which are indirectly but purposefully influenced by the policymaker.
3. Irrelevant variables, which measure side effects in which the policymaker is not interested.
4. Instrument variables, which are the means available to the policymakers for achieving their objectives and whose values are determined directly by them.
5. Data variables, which are subject to neither direct nor indirect control of the policymaker.
6. A quantitative model, which consists of empirical relationships among the variables.
7. Boundary conditions on the variables.

The solution to this model is a set of values of the instrument and target variables that satisfies the boundary conditions and the quantitative model and that maximizes (or minimizes) the objective function for given values of the data variables.

Useful though this theory is, we must keep in mind that it may be inadequate to handle problems that contain nonmeasurable, qualitative elements such as prestige or fairness.

Questions to consider. The list does not consist of mutually exclusive questions; e.g., the identification of target variables must be considered in answering the second, sixth, ninth, and tenth questions. In problem formulation, repetition is not necessarily redundancy. Sometimes the secret to successful problem formulation is to see the pieces of the problem in the right light. Looking at certain pieces in answer to one question may not be nearly as illuminating as looking at the same pieces in answer to another. Drucker (1970, p. 175) emphasized this: "To *know* something, to really understand something important, one must look at it from sixteen different angles." In searching for answers, we must be aware, as Ackoff (1978) has shown, of the dangers inherent in trying to understand the objectives of others, of believing that *they* should behave in accordance with *our* concept of rationality or efficiency, and of thinking that they cannot know what we do not know and cannot do what we cannot explain.

WHAT IS THE EXISTING SITUATION? A problem exists when someone is dissatisfied because of a deviation of the existing condition from the desired condition: what is differs from what ought to be. Part of the process of problem definition, then, is to identify and describe the existing situation. This question is so broad that it provides little guidance, but it reminds us that problem definition requires an understanding of prevailing circumstances.

WHO IS THE DECISION MAKER? Who is (are) the decision maker(s) you expect will use your research? A manager of a specific cooperative elevator? A sales manager? Perhaps there are several decision makers, all faced with a similar problem. They may be fellow scientists. In this situation it is appropriate to ask the questions about the people whose behavior is to be understood rather than about the particular decision maker(s) for whom your results are intended.

The question is couched in terms of users of your research, not in terms of beneficiaries, because you cannot be sure who will benefit from research until you know the outcome. And if you already know the outcome, there is no need to do the research.

WHAT ARE THE DECISION MAKER'S OBJECTIVES? What are the objectives of the decision maker(s) who will use your results? What are the target variables? Which one of the objectives do you need to consider in this project? Does your decision maker have an objective, welfare, or cost function—something that can be maximized or minimized? Perhaps the decision maker has a lexicographic utility function, or desires to minimize the cost of performing a specific operation or the likelihood of a wrong decision. Some target variables may be noneconomic, for example, prestige, number of votes in an election, fairness. Perhaps it is not possible or appropriate for you to specify an objective function to be maximized, but you can list several variables whose values do concern the decision maker. Even if a decision maker is not a maximizer, optimization analysis may provide information that helps to reach a decision. The mere statement of an optimization problem provides organized information on constraints, alternative available actions, costs, and benefits of available actions. Optimizing solutions can be manipulated to provide considerable information on feasible combinations of actions and marginal rates of substitution among alternatives.

You may not need to consider all of the decision maker's objectives; it may be sufficient for you to consider only one. In studying feasibility of use of the live cattle futures market by cattle feeders, it may be sufficient to assume that the feeder's objective is to maximize profit from each steer fed to slaughter weight. In another study of this same feeder it might be necessary to specify the objective to be maximization of total profit from all steers fed and all hogs raised. Many things that must be treated as variables in this latter study can be treated as constants or parameters in the first one.

WHICH DECISIONS? With which one or ones of the policymaker's decisions are you concerned? (This question is related to the previous one.) Are you concerned with a sales manager's decisions on quotas to assign to each salesperson? With the decision on how much point-of-purchase display material to allow each salesperson? Maybe you are concerned with a governor's decision on how much to raise the sales tax. Or perhaps you are concerned with the governor's decisions on sales, income, and property tax rates.

WHAT ARE THE AVAILABLE ACTIONS? What alternative actions are available for achieving the objectives? What are the decision maker's instrument variables? What carrots and what sticks? What can the decision maker do to make some actions, or the results thereof, so attractive that people will want to take them and to make alternatives A and B so highly unattractive that people will choose alternative C to avoid the outcomes from A and B? What are the requirements (resource, legal, policy, etc.) for the various actions?

WHAT ARE THE PARAMETERS? What are the parameters, the givens, or the given data? List, describe, and define them. These are taken as given in solving the problem. The values specified for them will affect your solution, but your solution will not affect their values.

WHAT ARE THE VARIABLES? What are the target variables? What are the instrument variables? Another way of asking this last question is, What means are available to the decision maker for reaching the objective? What are the irrelevant variables? Irrelevant variables have this name because the decision maker is indifferent to their values; they do not enter the objective function and are not subject to the control of the policymaker. But they are not irrelevant to the investigator. They must be included because they influence the values of the target variables or because their exclusion would bias statistical estimates of the quantitative model.

In addition to classifying variables according to the quantitative economic policy grouping, classify them according to econometric criteria as endogenous, exogenous, and predetermined. In this context, exogenous variables are like parameters in that both affect solution values of endogenous variables but are not affected by those values. Exogenous variables and parameters usually differ in that values of the former are observed, whereas values of the latter are estimated by some statistical method; and the former do not have the same value for all observations, whereas the latter do.

List, describe, and define the variables. The values of the variables will be determined by your analysis. Their values will be affected by those you assign the parameters but will not affect the parameter values. Obviously, your classification into variables and parameters is highly decision and objective oriented. Many things treated as parameters (or ignored) in a study of routing trucks to haul the milk produced by a dairy cooperative's members will be variables in a study whose objective is to determine how the cooperative can maximize the price its members receive for their milk.

Items classified as variables at one stage of a study may be classified as parameters in a later stage. A variable classified as endogenous for estimation purposes may be an instrument variable in a later stage.

WHAT ARE THE RELATIONSHIPS? What are the relationships of the problem? What are the relationships among the variables and the parameters? Can you express these relationships mathematically? Can you tabulate them? Graph them? The values of the variables will be determined by the relationships and the parameter values.

The preceding questions focus on individual components of the problem. They deal with analysis, determination of constituent parts. This question deals with synthesis, combining the parts into a whole.

Problem formulation requires identifying and describing the individual pieces of a problem and determining interrelationships among them. Unfortunately, much professional writing gives a misleading impression of the relative importance of analysis and synthesis. People commonly use the term "analyze" when they mean "study" or "investigate," that is, when they mean both "analyze and synthesize." Analysis is like dismantling an automobile engine. Synthesis is like putting the pieces back together so the engine works properly. Analysis of a car engine, by itself, will not show you how an engine works. This requires synthesis.

Many people find flow diagrams or flow charts helpful in synthesis. Fox (1958) presents flow charts of the demand and price structures for a dozen different agricultural commodities. Duesenberry et al. (1969) present a condensed flow diagram of the Brookings econometric model. Foote (1958) discusses use of flow charts or diagrams of supply-demand-price structures and presents flow charts of varying degrees of complexity. In their book on organizations, March and Simon (1958) make frequent use of flow charts. They present some sixteen in all, dealing with such diverse topics as models of organizational learning, factors affecting perceived consequences of evoked states of affairs, factors affecting perceived prestige of groups, and factors affecting intergroup conflict within an organization. Bonini's (1963) study of a business firm presents several flow charts dealing with formal organization, sales forecasting procedure, sales administrative expense budget, determination of the overall company plan, and changes in standards by the industrial engineering department.

One may also find it helpful to use an event graph (Mihram 1972, pp. 225–26) of directed arcs and nodes that indicate cause-and-effect relationships. Each node represents an event. We can use a solid arrow connecting two nodes to mean that one event causes or generates the other; a dashed arrow to indicate possible causation; a slashed solid arrow to mean that one event cancels the other; and a slashed, dashed arrow to signify possible cancellation.

WHAT RESTRICTIONS HAVE TO BE CONSIDERED? What restrictions limit the decision maker's actions or their outcomes? Do the parameters and the relationships, including the restrictions, provide enough information to let you determine the values of the variables? If we have adequately and correctly answered the preceding question on parameters, variables, and relationships, we will have at least partially (and perhaps completely) answered this question.

The restrictions may, as in the case of a linear program, enter the problem as constraints, or they may result from the behavior of others. To formulate these restrictions it may be necessary to consider the objectives of and limitations on these other people. A marketing vice-president who has decided that the best way to increase the number of units of Product X sold is to use a different package cannot carry out the decision if the production vice-president refuses to allow the different package to be produced. The restrictions may be self-imposed. The decision maker may refuse to take some actions, but may change his or her mind after measuring all the costs or the benefits foregone by virtue of the refusal.

Restrictions may enter a problem through the objective function. A firm's volume of sales, and hence its profit, may be affected by the price it charges. The propensity of consumers to reduce purchases as the price rises affects the volume sold at each price and limits revenue and profit. This is easily handled in a profit-maximizing problem by incorporating demand functions into the objective function.

WHAT OTHER DECISION MAKERS? In some cases the questions need to be asked about other decision makers as well as or instead of about the one(s) who will use your information. Perhaps the ones to whom you are providing information are educators or governmental bureaucrats who will use the information to help others achieve their objectives. Then you need to ask, Who are these others whom the educators or bureaucrats are trying to help? What are their objectives? What decisions are the educators or bureaucrats trying to help them with? What are the relevant parameters, variables, conditions, and restrictions that need to be taken into account to understand these other decision makers?

HAVE YOU SEEN SIMILAR PROBLEMS? Can you think of any similar problems that have been solved? Any simpler problems? Can you generalize this simpler problem? Can you think of any problems that are more complicated than yours that have been solved? Do you know of any problems having a similar list of variables? Of parameters? Of relations? Having a similar objective function? Similar restrictions? Concerned with the same decisions? Do you know of any problem having the same symptoms? The same causes? The related problem may treat as variables some of the items you consider to be parameters, and vice versa. Your problem and the related problem may have the same verbal description. Some of the variables, parameters, constraints, and objectives may have the same names in the two problems.

Two problems may have different verbal descriptions but the same mathematical description. An ability to recognize and to hypothesize mathematical structures is a tremendous aid in identifying, formulating, and solving problems.

This question brings to mind review of the literature. Professional journals, books, bulletins, trade publications, theses—all are places one might look for reports on similar problems. Unfortunately, many people approach review of the literature with the wrong expectation, that "somewhere in the literature I will find that someone has done my job for me; someone has provided exactly the problem formulation and research procedure that I need." This may turn out to be true, but you should not expect it to be. The purpose of reviewing the literature is not to find "the" formulation for your situation but to find some possibilities and to help you come up with an appropriate formulation, that is, not to find answers, but to find insights. The fact that someone (or several people) has formulated and studied a problem in one way is not by itself evidence that no better way exists. Beveridge (1957, p. 5) cites George Bernard Shaw's aphorism, "Reading rots the mind," to emphasize the dangers inherent in the necessary step of reviewing the literature. Increasing your knowledge of what others have done may blunt your own inventiveness. If you know too well what others have done in certain circumstances, you can be too easily convinced that is what you should do. This is especially true if you are "only a graduate student" and you have been studying the "experts."

What you fail to find in the literature may be more important than what you do find. The former helps you identify what has not been done. It is possible that what you need to do is something that no one has done before. This need not mean that what you need to do is more difficult than what others have done before.

By all means review the relevant literature. The difficulty with this advice lies in defining "relevant." You cannot be sure of knowing everything that is relevant until you know everything.

DOES A MODEL FIT? I know (or know about) Model (or analytical framework) M (for example, location model, Markov process). Does Model M fit my problem? Can I formulate my problem so that it fits Model M? Do the things I can take as parameters have the properties attributed to parameters in Model M? Do the entities I must treat as variables have the properties attributed to variables in Model M? Can Model M be used to express the restrictions and conditions I have imposed? Can I legitimately modify Model M so that it will fit my problem? Or can I legitimately modify my statement of the problem so that it will fit Model M? If the answers to the preceding questions are "no," what about Model N? How well does Model N fit the problem?

In considering these questions one must be leery of a quick "yes" answer before serious and critical consideration. An overreadiness to answer "yes" can lead to "cookbookery" and "mathematistry," to use Box's (1976, p. 797) terms. The symptoms of cookbookery are "a tendency to force all problems into the molds of one or two routine techniques, insufficient thought being given to the real objectives of the investigation or to the relevance of the assumptions of the imposed methods. . . . Mathematistry is characterized by the development of theory for theory's sake, which since it seldom touches down with practice, has a tendency to redefine the problem rather than solve it." Critical and judicious consideration of these questions, however, should help you clarify the nature of the variables, parameters, relations, and objectives in your study without leading you into cookbookery or mathematistry.

It can be helpful to attempt two or three different model expressions of the problem. Comparison of the different objective functions, the different lists of variables and parameters, and their relationships can provide valuable insight into the problem.

STOCHASTIC OR DETERMINISTIC? Is my problem purely stochastic? Purely deterministic? Or a mixture? The nature of the problem may be such that linear programming (deterministic) is appropriate. Another nearly identical problem may require the use of stochastic programming. Some models used for inventory control are stochastic because demand in each future month can only be expressed as a probability distribution. An inventory control model would, however, be strictly deterministic if demand in each future month could be expressed as a known function. A mixed model is another possibility: demand in each future month could be expressed as the sum of a known demand function and a random error term.

SOLVE A PROXY PROBLEM? It may not be possible to formulate or solve the problem that needs to be solved. It may be necessary to settle for solution of a proxy problem. A farm-supply cooperative may ask, Should we charge members high prices for supplies we sell them so that we can have large net savings and pay large patronage refunds to members at the end of the year? Or should we charge lower prices, have smaller net savings, and pay smaller patronage refunds? Perhaps we cannot answer this question because we cannot predict members' responses to variations in prices and refunds. But we may be able to interview members and nonmembers to determine the importance to them of prices and patronage refunds as methods of attracting their business and their membership.

USE REITERATION. Problem formulation is an iterative process. It will usually not be sufficient to ask and answer each question only once. Initial answers must be treated as tentative. In answering the third or the tenth question, you may discover something you overlooked in answering the first and be forced to revise your answer to it. The subsequent revision in your answer to the first question may show that you need to reconsider your answer to the fourth. Information you uncover after you have formulated the problem and started your research may show that you need to revise your formulation. Identifying the decision maker's objectives may be the most difficult step of all. And it is quite likely that answers to other questions will lead to modifying the description of that objective. A common, and unhappy, experience is to be forced to revise your problem formulation because of lack of data.

In some cases it is fruitful to imagine various solutions to a problem and then perform mental experiments on each and discuss it with the people facing the problem to discover its adequacies and inadequacies.

I now try to justify my assertion at the beginning of this section that the person whose sole motive is intellectual curiosity will find the above questions helpful. This person will need to ask these questions. Suppose you are trying to explain an observed phenomenon of human behavior. You will want to identify the decision makers whose behavior may account for the phenomenon, their objectives, and restrictions on their behavior. You will need to identify some things as variables and others as parameters and will need to consider the possible relationships among them. You will probably search the literature for explanations of similar phenomena (similar problems) or for explanations that may be adapted to explain your phenomenon (model fitting).

12 Tension

HAVE YOU EVER wanted an answer so badly that you hurt? Conscious absorption of a problem and an intense desire to know provide a strong stimulus to the unconscious. In discussing the creative person, Maslow (1967, p. 47) has written of "this total fascination with the matter-in-hand, this getting lost in the present, this detachment from time and place." Such total immersion in a problem bespeaks of intense concentration and overpowering desire for a solution. The stereotype of the absent-minded professor has a factual basis in the actual behavior of professors experiencing "this detachment from time and place" while in the throes of "tense thought," to use Hadamard's term (1954). This absent-mindedness can more correctly be called "single-mindedness," or "present-mindedness — present somewhere else." The person's mind has room for thoughts on only the one topic.

What are the sources of a strong desire for a solution? One is certainly curiosity. Heilbroner (1983, p. 13) wrote that one thing the great political economists shared was a common curiosity. And what is curiosity? For one thing, it is an expression of humanity's cognitive need: an urge to inquire, to explore. It seems to me that curiosity also has an aesthetic component: an intellectual aesthetic sense or a yearning for intellectual tidiness. Beveridge (1957, p. 77) wrote of the "love of order and logical connection between facts." As Polya (1957, p. 45) expressed it, "The feeling that harmonious simple order cannot be deceitful guides the discoverer both in the mathematical and in the other sciences." Imagine a human portrait in which the painter had left out the left eye and upper lip and had painted smooth skin in their places. Any such incomplete or broken pattern of facts and ideas or a pattern with discordant pieces will create an impression of ugliness, an aesthetic tension. When we finally do see the pattern complete and unbroken, we experience a delightful release of the tension. We perceive something soothing or delightful to our sense of intellectual aesthetics.

The mathematicians Poincare (1913, pp. 391–93) and Hadamard (1954, pp. 30–32) attribute great importance to aesthetic emotions as guides in mathematical invention. According to them, aesthetic emotions affect the selection of subjects for research, provide a drive toward discovery, and even determine which of the many possible answers created by unconscious activities will filter through to consciousness. Kuhn (1969, pp. 154, 156) has argued that during a scientific revolution, when a previously accepted paradigm is under attack by new ones, each individual's aesthetic sense will affect the choice of paradigm.

There have been times when I strongly believed something to be true when the main reason for believing it was only the feeling that something so beautiful and orderly must be true. Sometimes my aesthetic intuition has turned out to be correct; the "beautiful and orderly" answer was the correct one. At other times my aesthetic intuition was incorrect. What I had believed to be true because of its beauty turned out to be false in spite of it. Our intellectual aesthetic sense provides us two things: a desire to know and a criterion for judging results of our mental efforts.

I suspect that curiosity also has a component of the naive, open-eyed wonder of a child at the marvels of the world. The world is full of strange and marvelous things for me to see, feel, taste, hear, and try to understand.

Another source of strong desire for a solution may be the ego. Obtaining a solution gives one a sense of mastery. This source of strong desire may be especially relevant for teachers and lecturers. The answer "I don't know" is acceptable if used in moderation, but it is damaging to the ego (and likely also to one's career) to be forced to use it frequently.

I experience a tremendous sense of satisfaction whenever I discover something that no one has known before. I also experience a satisfying sense of accomplishment whenever I learn something that is new to me but has been known by others. Desire to experience the thrill of discovery provides a desire for a solution. "Nothing could please the creative person more than the act itself of doing, or having accomplished, his creative work" (Arieti 1976, p. 324). Drucker (1970, p. 168) writes that we know that "the only motivation we have for knowledge is achievement. Anybody who has ever had a great success is motivated from then on. It is a taste one never loses." And Beveridge (1957, p. 192) argues that the scientist's greatest reward is the thrill of discovery. Thus we can conclude that thrill of discovery is simultaneously a reward for past efforts and a motive for future ones.

Torrance and Myers (1970, p. 56) have written of "unforgettable experiences observing five-year-olds learn mathematics. After children have figured out the value of an unknown (the number of blocks under a box) in an equation and then checked their accuracy, the resulting wild glee is something to behold." I suspect that every scientist who has made an original discovery, no matter how minor, can empathize with the wild glee of these five-year-olds. The scientist has felt the same emotion, although probably expressed in a less uninhibited way. But Archimedes's "Eureka" response to his discovery of a way to determine if Hiero's crown was of pure gold or was adulterated with silver was an uninhibited expression of his joy.

A person who has never been cold cannot fully appreciate being warm. One of the great pleasures of ice-fishing is coming home to a hot meal in a warm house after spending several hours on a frozen lake. In the same way, a discovery that has been preceded by travail and frustration is made all the more marvelous by the tension and agonies of uncertainty and not knowing, and the discovery results in the same emotional high that the five-year-olds and Archimedes experienced.

In addition to experiencing the joy of discovery, the scientist may also experience a certain self-transcendent fulfillment. Concerning his thoughts and emotions immediately after one discovery, Austin (1978, p. 24) wrote, "To a biologist one of these thoughts was deeply gratifying. It seemed as though I would probably be worth my grain of salt on some eternal time scale. Our work had added one fact to the mass of information in the universe."

A person's desire for a solution may rise from a feeling of frustration with the inadequacies of present answers to a question or irritation over the lack of an answer.

In discussing preparation, Wallas (1926) has discussed the desirability of having a clear question in mind. A practice that relates to this and also helps to maintain intensity of purpose is a "treasure map." Bale (1979) wrote, "I have found that fantasizing is extremely helpful in supplementing my creativity. Sometimes I even draw a 'treasure map' of an event that I want to occur and write notes on it as if the event has occurred. I then hang the map in a prominent place where I can frequently see the goal that I am endeavoring to achieve." He finds that this serves to keep his thoughts focused. And, of course, it reminds him of his desired goal.

13 *Temporary abandonment*

ODDLY, sometimes the best thing to do when you are burning for an answer is to quit consciously trying to find one. A practice that most people find favorable to unconscious activity is temporary conscious abandonment of the problem. Upon returning to the problem later, they frequently find that they have acquired new ideas or insights in the interim. One undesirable result of overlong conscious pondering of a problem is conditioned thinking, which is like cycling in solving a degenerate linear program: the mind continually retraces the same established (and fruitless) patterns of thought. Temporary abandonment helps to break these fruitless patterns. The value of temporary abandonment is reflected in the old proverb, "Sleep on it."

The essence of Wallas's second stage in inventive thought (incubation) is temporary conscious abandonment. You may also temporarily abandon a problem during the preparation stage. You may alternate between conscious thought and temporary abandonment several times before finally coming up with a good solution.

One graduate student (who, as many do, worked many hours in late evenings) told me that when he was having difficulty he would concentrate on the problem for the last 15 to 30 minutes before going home and then not think about it any more that evening. The problem frequently would be clarified, if not solved, by the time he returned to his office the next morning. A colleague has told me that he works most effectively when engaged in intense concentration if he takes a five-minute break every half-hour. During that five minutes he may take a coffee break or walk to the water fountain for a drink. After the break he returns to work refreshed. His telling me this made me aware that I follow a similar pattern of behavior. After he had finished his Ph.D. dissertation, a former student of mine (Hauser 1981) wrote, "I have found it useful to follow a procedure in which I (1) make a decision concerning the means by which a job will be done, (2) defer the mechanics for a day or two, (3) consciously think about alternative means during the interim, and then (4) do the mechanics. In many cases other, better means will occur to me during the interim."

Hutchinson (1949) has pointed out the psychological value of temporarily abandoning work on a problem. Section 6 on stages of scientific invention mentioned his stage of frustration and suggested that frustration was not a stage but an emotion that might be experienced during any stage. Any strongly motivated creative worker (and no other kind is successful) inevitably experiences tensions. The sources are many and well known. Among them are hypotheses we were confident would lead to successful solutions, but did not; ideas that we hoped (and prayed) would succeed, but did not; stupid errors; reasonable errors, but nonetheless errors; felt sense (or fear) of inadequacy; feelings of futility and stupidity; fear of failure; thwarted ambition. If sufficiently numerous and prolonged, the tensions develop into frustration. No person can retain mental and emotional equilibrium in the face of continual failure and frustration. Hutchinson (1949, pp. 62–84) discusses various possible reactions, many of them pathological, and concludes that the most effective way to respond to frustration is to abandon the problem temporarily. Temporary abandonment thus has therapeutic value: one way to cure your headache is to stop beating your head against the wall. He also mentions another psychological justification for temporary abandonment (p. 139). Psychologists have found that properly spaced periods of learning are more effective than continuous effort.

MacKinnon (1966, p. 183) writes of "flexible endurance" or "flexible persistence" of highly creative individuals, who are "much more ready [than less creative individuals] to recognize the fact that they are blocked and turn to something else . . . , then come back to the task later." Although highly creative people are single-minded, they are not bullheaded. They are willing to set the problem aside for a time. But they persist in returning to it later.

One may temporarily abandon conscious efforts on one problem to turn the conscious mind to others. But one may also temporarily abandon conscious efforts on all research. Most people find a period of relaxation or light effort (driving, showering, walking) immediately following a period of serious effort to be a favorable time for intuitions. Some individuals find the time of drowsiness that precedes full sleep to be a favorable time for intuitions. The unconscious processes of some people are active at night, and they will be awakened during the night by bright ideas. These people need to have paper and pencil or recorder handy.

Hutchinson (1949, pp. 123–28) presents testimony from a number of people in creative fields (including mathematics) that they dream frequently about their work and often obtain useful ideas and sometimes even solutions from their dreams. Some people find lying in bed in the morning just after waking or while half-awake to be favorable to appearance of intuitions. Others find a combination of mental relaxation and physical exercise to be conducive. Some find background music helpful.

Arieti (1976, p. 374) argued that one condition that seems to promote creativity is inactivity: taking time to "do nothing" but speculate, cogitate, daydream, let your mind roam freely, satisfy your curiosity. Hutchinson (1949) agrees and refers to this as "masterful idleness."

14 *Writing*

YOUNG (1951, p. 1) wrote, "The scientist does not usually think of the writing of books or preparing of lectures as research. Writing seems to him to be a rather tiresome labour that he must do after the fun of laboratory research and discovery is over." This seems to me, unfortunately, to express many persons' attitude toward writing: they see it only as a research-reporting tool and overlook its value as a research tool. But later on in the same paragraph, Young came closer to expressing my own attitude toward writing: "I came to realize the extent to which having to describe the results of one's thoughts to others is a part of the process of discovery itself."

Many of my intuitions come to me when I am writing. It frequently is true that I do not know what I think until I write it. It sometimes happens, for example, that I start to write a paragraph knowing only the first sentence and having only a vague idea of the central theme. But by the time I have written that first sentence, the second is composed in my mind; by the time that sentence is written, the ideas to be expressed in the next two sentences are clear in my mind. And at the end of the paragraph I will have expressed some ideas that I did not have at the start, or at least did not know I had. Writing is frequently an adventure. At first I know only the first step and do not know where I will end until I get there. (It occurs to me that this sentence describes the attraction of research. When you start, you do not know where you will end, but getting there is fun.) For completeness, I need to add that the paragraph containing ideas that I did not know when I started almost never reaches my secretary's desk but ends up in the wastebasket. Sometimes this happens because the ideas are incomplete, incoherently expressed, or out of order. Sometimes they are irrelevant or wrong. Even the latter outcome is usually valuable because it has started a flow of ideas, some of which do turn out to be useful.

Clardy (1977) beautifully expressed my attitude toward writing:

I have acquired many things by writing them. There are allegedly those who know what they have to say before saying it, but I have never counted myself in their number. Argument seems to be a means of developing rather than merely demonstrating theories, and articulation a means of amassing rather than just disseminating insight. Writing is as much the cause as the result of having something to say.

Poets, novelists, and other intellectual workers have ascribed some of their inventions to some such spontaneous or automatic activity as I experience at times in my writing. Ernst (1952, p. 59) has written, "The author is present as a spectator . . . at the birth of his own work, and observes the phases of his own development." Note the phraseology: the author "observes" the development but does not consciously control it. Nietzsche (1952, p. 209) puts it dramatically: "Provided one has the slightest remnant of superstition left, one can hardly reject completely the idea that one is the mere incarnation, or mouthpiece, or medium of some almighty power."

In a discussion of the psychology of problem solving and insight, Hilgard and Bower (1975, p. 273) write, "Insight is more likely when the problematic situation is so arranged that all necessary aspects are open to observation. Moreover, solution occurs more quickly if all the parts which need to be brought into relationship are simultaneously present in perception. . . ." This provides a strong argument for starting your writing at an early stage of an investigation. For most of us it is not possible to have all necessary aspects open to observation and simultaneously present in perception if they are stored only in our mind. The only way we can be sure that all parts of the situation are perceived and open to observation and organized is to have them inventoried in an organized write-up. Imagery seems to perform the same function for some mathematicians that writing performs for us; see Hadamard (1954, Ch. 6).

The experience of learning from your own writing does not end at the first draft. In discussing rewriting and restating the evidence, Penfield (1970, p. 106) states, "Often, once I get my thoughts truly expressed, I see things I never suspected before." And this leads to another possibility. Sometimes your thoughts can be truly expressed in different ways, each way suggesting different insights. To be able to express something in different ways or to perceive the same thing from different perspectives is valuable at any stage of research; perhaps at no time is this truer than during the preparation stage.

Writing is a part of the process of discovery. We sometimes find out in this writing-discovery process that we know something, but not clearly or completely. A symptom of this is difficulty with a sentence. An unclear sentence may reflect inability to express a clear thought, or it may accurately express an unclear thought. In this latter circumstance we must clarify our thoughts before we can clarify our sentence. Writing helps us to find out what we know clearly and what we know vaguely. In the preparation stage this function of writing helps us identify areas where we are not fully prepared. In the verification stage this function tests the idea's readiness for use, and our readiness to use it, and prepares us to use the idea. During verification, we make precise the results of one illumination. Except for simple results that are easily comprehended in a single glance, this requires written expression. This in turn serves as preparation for another effort. According to these arguments writing is useful in the preparation, incubation, illumination, and verification stages of invention.

Koestler (1975, pp. 173–77) wrote of "the snares of language." One snare is that words have specific meanings, which may poorly or inaccurately convey the significance of an image or idea. This may account for the fact that some ideas or thoughts can be expressed in several ways, but no one way is completely satisfactory because none conveys all essential elements of the thought. A related snare is to lose some of the richness of a perception when it is translated into words and to confuse the words with the perceptions.

We must not overlook the fact that writing plays different roles in different stages of research. During intense concentration, for example, your writing is likely to consist of scribbling, a personal shorthand statement of key steps and keywords. Thus the statement "When price of product one rises sharply, consumption of product one falls sharply because of a high price elasticity of demand, and consumption of product two increases slightly because of a low cross-price elasticity of demand" becomes "$P_1 \uparrow \rightarrow Q_1 \downarrow$ & $Q_2 \nearrow$."

We usually think of writing as something that we do to report results to others. What is being advocated here is writing to yourself to generate or discover knowledge to "discover what [you] know by the deliberate activity of knowing it" as Middleman and Blaylock (1983, p. 7) put it in an article advocating the use of writing assignments to increase students' understanding of quantitative methods. This position is similar to the one you have probably heard (and may have expressed yourself): "The best way to learn something is to have to teach it." For some statistical support for this view, see Siegfried

(1977). He concluded that proctoring an introductory economics course significantly improves the student proctor's understanding of economics principles.

Writing out in detail the statement of the problem, how you plan to solve it, and why you plan to solve it in the way you do can save work and help to avoid embarrassment. Have you ever had this experience? You write a report of what you have done; someone questions why you did a particular thing in the certain way that you did and, further, suggests an alternative way. Upon reflection you decide the alternative is superior to the one you used, and the only justification you can find for your method is that "it seemed like a good idea at the time?" I experienced this and similar embarrassments a number of times before I finally learned to think carefully (and for me, this means to write) before doing my empirical work. My habit has been for some years now to write up my research before actually doing it. Doing so has saved me from many stupid mistakes.

For the past several years I have required each student who is writing a thesis under my direction to write his or her thesis before doing the research. Before beginning to collect and analyze data, the student is to prepare a report covering the statement of the problem, review of literature, theoretical analysis (economic, statistical, econometric, or operation research), data used, method of data collection, and method of empirical analysis of the data: everything but results, summary, and conclusions. This causes the student to solve many problems before they ever arise and to solve them in a consistent, coherent way. Also, it reduces the collection of unnecessary data, likelihood of failure to collect needed data, number of false starts, and performance of unneeded computations.

In practice the alternative to having students write their theses before doing the research is to have them doing and deciding simultaneously. While doing the research, they are also deciding how to do research. A common result is that doing gets ahead of thinking and, when they finally begin to think about what was done last week, they discover that it was done wrong; that work has to be thrown out and done in a different way. Access to electronic computers handicaps the student, or any other researcher, who tries to plan and perform research simultaneously. If students try to keep the computer busy, and many seem to feel the need to do so, their own busyness keeps them from doing adequate planning.

A common objective of research is the testing of hypotheses. Before you ever start testing, you ought to know which hypotheses you will test, how you will test them, why you will test them, and how you will interpret the results. Writing a report before doing the research increases your chances of knowing these things and, consequently, of correctly performing and interpreting the tests of hypotheses that are most relevant for the problem. Every research project involves use of maintained hypotheses, that is, of things that are assumed to be true for the purposes and duration of the study. Sometimes the question of whether a specific hypothesis should be tested or maintained can be critical. Recognizing the critical nature of the decision and reaching a proper conclusion are more likely to occur if you write before you act. Also, the hypotheses to be tested and the manner of testing them are critically dependent on the choice of maintained hypotheses.

Another thing that I encourage students to do before doing their research (but do not require) is to prepare a mock write-up of their results: determine (1) the order in which the results will be presented, (2) the points to be covered, (3) the number and titles of graphs and tables (including row stubs and column headings), and (4) the nature of interpretations to be placed on the results.

Another reason for having a student do the writing early is this. Public funds are assigned to me and I am responsible for them. When a student is spending those funds to gather data or perform computations, I feel much more comfortable if I know what the student is doing and if I am confident that the student knows how to do it.

Austin (1978, p. 171) presents an excellent reason for doing the writing before the research is completed. He writes, "The investigator must finally put all the information into a manuscript for publication complete with tables, figures, and bibliography, and must try to anticipate which editors of which journals will be the most receptive. By now, . . . *months* have gone by. The original ideas have lost their luster. Completing the manuscript is like giving birth to a cactus that has bloomed long before." Writing is much less painful if done as an early step in research than if left to the end.

Penfield's (1970, p. 6) quotation also provides a reason for writing early instead of late. The former allows time for you to "see things you never suspected before," including errors; the latter does not.

Apparently the process of trying to collect, organize, and express my thoughts stimulates my unconscious. Perhaps this is also one reason why many of my intuitions come when I am in discussion with colleagues or students; whether concerning their problems, my problems, or our problems.

15 *Exchange with colleagues*

DISCUSSION with others can be helpful in various ways. Your colleagues' or students' questions or comments can bring out points you had missed. They may present a new perspective that helps you to see the problem in a different way and provides new insight. They may point out an incorrect assumption you were making and show you a correct alternative. They may complete a partial idea of yours, or you may be able to complete a partial idea of theirs. They may verbalize a previously unexpressed hunch of yours. And sometimes, oddly enough, insights into your own problem are obtained by discussing a colleague's or student's problem. A psychological principle comes into play here. Verbalization of your ideas creates verbal imagery, which is of value in raising your thoughts from your unconscious to your conscious mind.

Discussion has other values in addition to the stimulus it provides to the unconscious. We need to remember what Keynes wrote (1936, p. vii): "It is astonishing what foolish things one can temporarily believe if one thinks too long alone." Discussion with colleagues provides a useful, but not infallible, defense against believing foolish things. Take care, however, lest your colleagues teach you foolish things that you did not know before.

Some people find that reading stimulates their unconscious. An obvious thing to do is to read papers or books dealing with problems similar to yours. If you are working on a formal research project, you may find it helpful to reread the project statement: problem, objectives, and procedures. Reading reports on topics unrelated to your problem may give you a new insight or an idea for a new method of organization or analysis. Scientific papers written by people with whom you disagree can be stimulating as well as irritating. Hofstadter (1979, p. 751) wrote of one book, "I am intrigued by books which seem wrong to me, yet in a hard-to-pin-down way," and of another (p. 754), "well-written, thought-provoking — sometimes infuriating —

book." Once in a while we all need to read books that are wrong in an elusive way or are infuriating. Reading such books stretches the mind. Attempts to identify what is wrong lead to new insights. If we consider the infuriating books honestly, we sometimes conclude that we were wrong and the infuriating book was right, and we are momentarily even more infuriated. If we conclude that the infuriating book was wrong, we end with a more complete understanding of our own position than we had before.

Some people find the most stimulating exchange with colleagues to be the exchange that occurs in a "pressurized environment," as when presenting and defending a paper before a friendly but critical audience. These people commonly say, "I think better on my feet."

The difference between writing and exchange with colleagues is that writing represents an exchange with one's self.

16 *Freedom from distraction*

ANOTHER CONDITION favorable to the unconscious is freedom from distraction: interruption by students or co-workers, intrusive noises, or pressures to be working on several other jobs in addition to the one currently occupying you. Intrusive influences that distract the conscious mind seem to inhibit the operation of the unconscious mind. These influences also make it more likely that ideas generated by the unconscious will be overlooked by the conscious.

It is a common experience that putting in eight hours on a research project in one eight-hour stretch or two four-hour stretches is much more productive than eight one-hour stretches. I think part of the explanation is this law of unconscious inertia: an unconscious in motion tends to stay in motion in the same direction. Time and effort are required to start the unconscious in motion in a given direction. But after it is moving, further time and effort are required to bring it to a stop and to start along a new line of thought. Each time you change jobs you must redirect your unconscious. Changing from one job to another shortly after the first is initiated requires that your unconscious be redirected before it has time to accomplish anything on the original.

In addition, frequent changes of direction make it difficult for the unconscious mind to thoroughly absorb any single problem. One might say that prolonged concentration on a problem permits the conscious to transmit information to the unconscious. When you change jobs frequently, the information transmitted from the conscious is received by the unconscious as random noise.

Littlefield (1978, p. 117) wrote of the need for warming up because "most people need half an hour or so before being able to concentrate fully." You have probably noticed that sometimes after you are warmed up new insights come in a steady stream, sometimes so rapidly you can hardly record them all. Frequent changing of jobs will sharply reduce the frequency with which you have these streams of insights.

Distraction is not only a matter of environment, it is also a matter of response to environment. In fact, it is more a matter of the second than the first. I have known students who were distracted from their work if an office door slammed clear over on the other side of the campus. These students have failed to acquire the mental discipline needed for learning techniques and practicing skills, and for logical thinking, creativity, and diligent effort. Arieti (1976, pp. 378–79) lists discipline as one of the necessary conditions for creativity.

Even though several jobs need your attention, that will be a distraction only if you let it be. You can prevent this by exercising a mental discipline that allows you to concentrate your efforts whole-heartedly on one job at a time. When some people are faced with three jobs that need to be done "soon," they concentrate on one and ignore the others until that one is finished or until they can make no more progress on it. Then they work on the second while ignoring the third. And finally they finish the third. They find that in this way they complete all three more quickly than if they try to treat them all equally and do a bit on each one every day.

Arieti (1976, p. 373) lists "aloneness" as one of the conditions for fostering creativity: freedom from distraction, external stimuli, and noise, and an ability to remain alone for a few hours. One pressing need that creative workers have is for time for preparation, verification, and reporting. But more importantly they need time for leisurely reflection and contemplation, mulling over ideas, and defining new problems; time for looking at a problem from every possible angle; time to test various possibilities, to dredge the unconscious for possible clues or links or cues, to speculate, to be curious, to verify that the problem has been properly identified and that nothing important was overlooked; time to free-associate ideas, to daydream, to follow their curiosity wherever it leads. Interrupting this kind of intellectual activity to prepare your report to the National Science Foundation is distraction just as surely as breaking off your preparation of a lecture to attend a committee meeting.

Even, or perhaps especially, in an academic environment, time for imaginative thinking is hard to find. Generally you will not have time for it unless you place it high on your list of priorities. Feynman (1983, pp. 13–14) reported:

To do the kind of high, real good physics work, you do need absolute solid lengths of time . . . it needs a lot of concentration—that is, solid time to think—and if you've got a job in administrating anything like that, then you don't have the solid time. So I have invented another myth for myself: that I'm irresponsible. I'm actively irresponsible. I tell everybody I don't do anything. If anybody asks me to be on a committee to take care of admissions, "No, I'm irresponsible. I don't give a damn about the students." Of course I give a damn about the students, but I know that somebody else'll do it. And I take the view, "Let George do it,"—a view which you're not supposed to take, okay, because that's not right to do. But I do that because I like to do physics and I want to see if I can still do it. And so I'm selfish, okay, I want to do my physics.

Hutchinson (1949, p. 81) warns us that "the attainment of this masterful idleness is in fact the hardest part of the creative discipline." Sometimes it seems to me that we are so busy that we do not have time to think. We are so busy being busy because we think that this is either a sign of being important or guarantees being productive. We do not dare take the time to do two jobs well because we must do five jobs passably to meet the demands placed upon us by students, colleagues, department heads, and deans. I am reminded of the plaintive poster behind the secretary's desk in the busy department head's office: "How come we never have time to do anything right, but we always have time to do it over?"

Both temporary abandonment and distraction mean changing the course of one's conscious thoughts. What is the difference between them? The essential difference is that one is voluntary and the other is involuntary. If you do it to yourself, it is temporary abandonment. If I do it to you, it is distraction.

⅏ 17 *Sensitivity to similarities*

ARIETI (1976, pp. 409–10) includes "a state of readiness for catching similarities" on his list of creativity-promoting conditions. Analogical reasoning is so important in discovery that, according to Koestler (1975, p. 200), "Some writers identify the creative act in its entirety with the unearthing of hidden analogies." Koestler argues that this statement does not carry quite the correct connotation. Unearthing of hidden analogies suggests that the analogies already existed. If they did, where were they hidden? The very meaninglessness of that question leads me to agree with Koestler that the unearthed analogy is a new invention of the creator's mind.

A common type of new invention is the perception or creation of a link between things that were not previously connected in any way. Often the link is an analogy, or it is suggested by an analogy. Two definitions of analogy are as a relation of likeness consisting in the resemblance not of the things themselves but of two or more attributes, circumstances, or effects and as a form of inference in which it is reasoned that if two (or more) things agree with one another in one or more respects they will probably agree in yet other respects. Analogical reasoning consists in hypothesizing that things alike in known ways are also alike in yet unknown ways.

Reasoning by analogy may help you to discover unknown relationships or unknown entities (see Fig. 17.1). Let AR_iB denote a particular relation between A and B. AR_iB and CR_iD means that the same relation that exists between A and B also exists between C and D. Consider boxes 1 and 2 where R_7 indicates a perceived analogy between the two. Box 2 is similar to box 1 in so many ways that analogy suggests the existence of a relation GR_5H in box 2 to correspond to CR_5D in box 1. Here analogy suggests the existence of a relationship. Now compare boxes 2 and 3. The analogy between these two is not so strong as that between boxes 1 and 2, but does suggest the existence of an item M in box 3 that satisfies JR_3M and KR_6M.

Here analogy suggests the existence of a new item.

Polya (1957, pp. 37–46; 1954, Ch. 2) demonstrates uses of analogy in heuristic reasoning and discusses the role of analogy in mathematical discovery. In a widely quoted lecture, Poincare (1913, pp. 386–87) has described his deliberate use of conscious analogy with

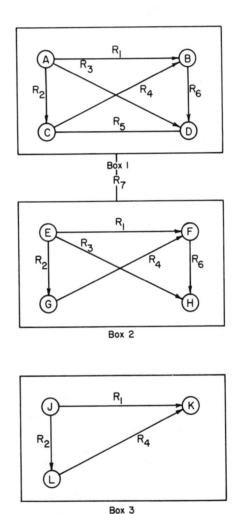

17.1.   *Examples of analogy.*

elliptic functions in his work on Fuchsian functions. He makes several references to use of analogies in mathematics and physics (pp. 151, 370-73, 379, 381). Bell (1937, p. 59) has described how the inventors of the calculus relied on geometric, kinematic, and dynamic intuition to make progress. Montmasson (1932, pp. 73-76) describes Laplace's use of analogy in the development of his astronomy. Kepler (see Koestler 1964, p. 125) used an analogy between the sun, the fixed stars, and the space between them on the one side and the Father, Son, and Holy Ghost on the other to guide his astronomical researches. This may seem to be a weak and strained analogy to you and me (whether it was a weak or a strong analogy to Kepler's contemporaries, I have no idea). But your analogy does not have to make sense to me for it to lead you to fruitful results. Koestler (1964, pp. 121-24) and Montmasson (1932, pp. 171-77) describe Gutenberg's uses of analogy in the invention of the printing press. Computer scientists and psychologists use analogies between human minds and computers, but for quite different purposes. Computer scientists use the analogy to further their understanding of computers. Psychologists use it to aid their understanding of the operation of human minds. Hilgard and Bower (1975, Ch. 13) summarize psychologists' information-processing theories of behavior. Section 3 discusses some uses of analogy in economics.

Analogical reasoning is valuable but highly fallible. We are likely to find that box 3 contains no item M but does contain item N, which satisfies LR_7N and NR_8K. Cookbookery is one consequence of seeing a complete analogy where only an incomplete analogy exists.

The new link between previously unconnected things may be provided by metaphor, which uses a word or phrase literally denoting one kind of object or idea in place of another by way of suggesting a likeness between them, as for example, using "empty-headed" to mean "thoughtless." The synectics method of group problem solving puts great emphasis on metaphorical thinking (Prince, 1970). McCloskey (1983, pp. 502-8) argues that economics is metaphorical. Among the metaphors that he cites are human capital, the auctioneer in general equilibrium theory, production function, and game theory.

The definitions of analogy and metaphor use the term "likeness." "Likeness" or "sameness" is not a property of things. It is a consequence of our perceptions, a property of our attributions. It is a product of human thought.

This book opened with the proposition that we scientists need to learn to use our subconscious minds so that we may be more productive of new ideas. I am now ready to assert my agreement with Warnock (1976) that we can have no knowledge of the world without imaginative sensitivity to similarities. Warnock (1976, p. 30) summarizes her position on the role of imagination in perception thus: "Without imagination we could never apply concepts to sense experience. Whereas a wholly sensory life would be without any regularity or organization; a purely intellectual life would be without any real content." The senses and the intellect "need a further element to join them. The joining element is the imagination. . . ." Also, "Imagination is our means of interpreting the world, and it is *also* our means of forming images in the mind. The images themselves are not separate from our interpretations of the world; they are our way of thinking of the objects in the world" (p. 194). Imagination connects things known in two different ways, by intellect and by senses.

Without the ability to imagine metaphors and analogies — to perceive likenesses between our concepts and our physical world — we would have no scientific knowledge of the world. Reading McCloskey (1983, pp. 502–8) and Jaynes (1977, Chs. 1, 2) on consciousness, language, and metaphor reinforces my agreement with Warnock. So does the logician Rosser's (1953, p. 10) statement that "a formal system is merely a model devised by human minds to represent some facts perceived intuitively."

To further justify my agreement with Warnock, let us step back and ask, What is knowledge? Where is it found? Knowledge is not found in libraries. Libraries contain only symbols that, if properly encoded and decoded, convey knowledge from one mind to another. Knowledge exists only in minds. Minds cannot contain concrete things like "consumers" or "automobiles." Minds contain only abstractions. (Note that even here we are thinking metaphorically. In what sense does a mind contain anything?) For science to exist there must be connections between the abstractions of the mind and the existential entities of the real world. How do we construct these connections? By using our imaginations to create likeness, that is, to create "epistemic correlations," in Northrop's (1959) terms. For example, in using linear programming to study a net-revenue-maximizing firm, we see similarities between c_j, x_j, a_{ij}, a_{i0}, activities, and their postulated properties on the one hand and such things as labor, land, stocks of fixed resources, variable inputs, and so forth, on the other. I see no other explanation than analogy and metaphor for our ability to label the symbol x_i in a linear program of a farm operation as "amount of corn produced." The ink mark x_i is itself a concrete representation of an idea or concept — activity level — that exists only in the mind and has a number of (abstract) properties or restrictions, for example, continuity and independence. It is also a symbol for "amount of corn produced." What permits us to believe that in the ways important to us "amount of corn produced" behaves like or has the properties of the concept "activity level"? The only mental faculty that we have for creating similarities between the concept "activity level," the symbol x_i, and the concrete "amount of corn produced" is our faculty for seeing similarities — analogy, metaphor, allegory — between unlike things.

Neither deductive, inductive, nor retroductive logic provides the connections. Logic consists of abstractions. Scientific arguments use the connections that are created by prelogical mental operations. (By prelogical, I mean prior to demonstrative logic. Construction of the connections is not illogic or unreason, but it is not subject to rules of demonstrative logic.) The connections are provided by imaginative perception that uses analogy and metaphor to create similarities between reality and the abstractions of the mind.

Perhaps we should add "awareness of connections" to "sensitive to similarities." Various people have observed how important it is to notice things, to be a good noticer. It does no good to be exposed to a solution if you do not notice it. It is no help to have an idea that will solve a problem if you are not aware that there is a problem or that you have a solution. It seems to help us to notice things if we "connect, connect, always connect," that is, if we try to relate everything we observe and learn to other things we know. (What you observe may relate by contradiction. Observing something that you did not expect can lead to a whole new insight, a new solution, or an absorbing new problem.) The things worth noticing may be novel or familiar. Sometimes perceiving in a new way something you have been in the presence of for years can lead to new discovery.

The discussion of model fitting in Section 11 is relevant to this section. An ability to recognize and to hypothesize mathematical and logical patterns is a great aid to problem formulation and also to finding similarities. This ability must be accompanied by an imaginative ability to connect the mental constructs of the patterns to the world of experience.

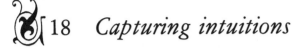

18 *Capturing intuitions*

IT DOES YOU no good to have a fertile unconscious if your conscious fails to grasp the results of your unconscious processes. Intuitions sometimes appear as pale shadows on the far edges of the conscious, and willful effort is required to grasp them before they are lost. You need to be alert to grasp these intuitions as soon as they appear. Commonly, an intuition lost once is lost permanently. Some people wisely make a habit of jotting down notes as their intuitions appear. People who are awakened at night by intuitions should have paper and pencil or recorder handy. It is frustrating to have a good idea come to mind shortly after going to bed, to decide, "I do not want to crawl out of bed and go to my desk to write this down, I will remember this and write it down in the morning," and then to be unable to remember or recreate the idea next morning. I have tried to develop a habit of writing down my intuitions immediately after they come to me. If I become aware of an intuition when I am working, I write it down immediately. If an intuition occurs to me after going to bed, I try to convince myself to arise and write it down. When an idea comes to mind while I am walking between home and office, I stop and jot it down immediately.

Sometimes you may fail to capture an idea because you suffer from an embarrassment of riches. One intuition after another comes tumbling into your conscious at such a rate that you cannot record them all as they appear. At such a time perhaps the best you can do is to jot down some key words, phrases, and incomplete sentences and then shortly come back and express each idea fully after the flow has ceased but before you have had time to forget what each key word or phrase was intended to represent.

Perhaps the best procedure is to live in a state of perpetual expectancy: to expect good ideas to appear at any time. It is not humanly possible to achieve this state, unfortunately, but one can strive for it.

For some people, illumination is preceded by intimation: a signal that warns that an illumination is coming but does not identify its nature. These people can be prepared to grasp the intuition as it appears.

19 Combinations

THE COMBINATIONS that are most stimulating to the unconscious are those that combine a number of the individual conditions presented here. One of my colleagues follows an interesting and highly successful, at least for him, pattern in his research. This pattern provides a regular schedule for many of the conditions discussed: preparation, incubation, writing, exchange with colleagues, verification, and avoidance of distractions. Whether this pattern would be useful for you can be determined only by you. He works on a topic for about six weeks, then writes a report, and then moves on to work on another topic for about six weeks. He gives copies of his report to colleagues for their evaluation and suggestions. On average, four to five months elapse between the time he quits working on a topic and the time he returns to it. When he does return, he may spend some time in reading. He certainly will do so if reviewers of his report have suggested further references or if he has found some relevant literature since last working on the subject. Upon returning to a problem, he critically evaluates his previous work, tests it, improves it if possible, incorporates new materials or ideas, carries toward completion work initiated but not completed, initiates work on new dimensions or aspects of the problem, and finally prepares another report.

This pattern allows him to concentrate exclusively on one job at a time while relieving him from worry about forgetting any of his previous work. It provides him a systematic way of exchanging knowledge with colleagues. The scheduled writing assures him of regularly reporting to (and learning from) himself what he knows. The report thus prepares him for future work. The four- to five-month interim period allows for incubation of new ideas.

I mentioned that writing can be an adventure in discovery for me. It usually has to be interspersed with periods of temporary abandonment while I digest, sort out, complete, reconcile, and synthesize separate ideas and obtain some insight into where they are leading me. Sometimes this temporary abandonment lasts no longer than three or four minutes, just long enough for me to go down the hall to the water fountain and look out the window for a minute.

One of life's enduring frustrations comes when you are anxious to work on a problem but current responsibilities do not allow you time—as during a spring semester when you have a heavy teaching load and also serve on committees whose final reports are due by the end of the semester, and all the while you are consumed with impatience to study the distribution of the solution to a quadratic program whose coefficients are statistical estimates.

One helpful trick is to work on the problem without taking time to work on it. Label a folder "problem X" (or whatever is appropriate) and place it in your file. If you are truly anxious to work on the problem, ideas will come to mind from time to time even when you are not consciously thinking about it. Every time an idea occurs to you, write it down and place your note in the file. The ideas may come from anywhere at any time: while reading on problem Y, you may see a similarity to problem X; while studying method A, it may occur to you that this method might be used on problem X. You might remember something you had learned and forgotten. Whatever the insight and wherever it comes from, record and file it. Do not try to evaluate it. Today's insight may contradict yesterday's. Do not reconcile them. After all, evaluation and reconciliation are conscious work, and you do not have time for conscious work on X. Also, right now you are not trying to solve X, you are only collecting ideas on possible ways to study it. Other things that should go into the file are clippings or copies of materials that strike you as relevant. When the semester finally ends, you will have collected enough material to get you off to a good start. You may even find that you have the solution to X in the file. At any one time you will have several problem files because you will have several problems that you want or intend to work on in the future but lack time for now.

The same strategy can be applied when you do not want to work on a problem that you do need to pursue. This strategy allows you to work on the problem without ever having to make the painful decision to begin. The conscious decision to begin will finally be made much easier by the existence of the file of notes.

PART III
The inevitability of luck

THERE IS ample evidence that research is affected by chance. Understanding the different kinds of chance and the psychology of problem solving increases the frequency with which chance brings good luck. Chance and problem solving are the subjects of the next two sections.

20 Chance

IT MIGHT SEEM surprising to treat luck or chance as research tools, but the mathematician Polya writes, "The first rule of discovery is to have brains and good luck" (1957, p. 172). Hadamard has also asserted that chance plays a role in mathematical discovery by intervening in the subconscious mental activities (1954, pp. 29, 30). Beveridge (1957, p. 55) has written, "New knowledge very often has its origin in some quite unexpected observation or chance occurrence arising during an investigation. The importance of this factor [chance] in discovery should be fully appreciated and research workers ought deliberately to exploit it." Beveridge demonstrates the importance of chance in research by presenting some thirty examples of discoveries in which chance played a key role (pp. 215–25). Among them are the discoveries of immunization with attenuated pathogens, a method of staining bacteria, electric current, the relation between electricity and magnetism, penicillin, X rays, and selective weed killers.

Nelson (1970, p. 256) reports:

There is also a story I'm very fond of. It's a story about Pasteur who was greatly envied by his colleagues and friends after he discovered the tuberculosis bacillus. He was very often given evidence of the acute jealousy of people in his or in related fields. My story has to do with a big reception at which Pasteur was the guest of honor. At this reception, one of his colleagues came up and said, "Isn't it extraordinary these days how many scientific achievements of our century are arrived at by accident?" Pasteur said, "Yes, it really is remarkable when you think about it, and furthermore did you ever observe to whom the accidents happen?

Pasteur's response becomes more meaningful if you know that he believed that "chance favors only the prepared mind." To say that chance favors *only* the prepared mind is to say that preparation is a necessary condition for fortunate accidents or that fortunate accidents do not happen to you if your mind is not prepared. For this reason, good luck is not a sufficient explanation of chance discoveries. The chance discovery resulted from the discoverer's ability to perceive a universal relation in a particular incident, that is, from the noticing of a connection.

It is not by chance that chance affects the outcome of many investigations. The effect of chance is more likely to be significant and beneficial if we have prepared minds and understand how to court Lady Luck. If we look at Austin's (1978) classification of chance and at psychologists' findings from their studies of problem solving, we will see that it is inevitable that research is affected by chance events.

Austin (1978) finds four kinds of chance that play roles in creative research. Having some understanding of their nature and the conditions under which they occur will help us to convert random events into lucky accidents and increase the number of lucky accidents. Chance 1 represents blind luck, completely accidental, completely independent of the investigator's own personality traits. You might call it pure dumb luck.

In chance 2, good luck is the result of general exploratory behavior. Its major premise is that "chance favors those in motion" (1978, p. 78) or "*un*luck runs out if you persist" (1978, p. 73). Its main feature is nonspecific exploratory actions in various directions in a promising area. Its obverse is that you will never stumble across something useful while sitting still.

In chance 3, good luck is the result of personal sagacity. It occurs to the prepared mind to which Pasteur referred. It results from a "background of knowledge, based on your abilities to observe, remember, and quickly form significant new associations" (1978, p. 78). In chance 3, "some special receptivity born from past experience permits you to discern a new fact or to perceive ideas in a new relationship" (1978, p. 78). Judson did not use the term, but he (1980, p. 194) was thinking of chance 3 when he wrote, "More often than not, a discovery is made by the worker who possesses a combination of knowledge that nobody else can muster" (another expression of the value of diversity!). Austin classifies chances 1, 2, and 3 as serendipity, "the facility for encountering unexpected good luck as the result of accident, sagacity or general exploratory behavior" (1978, p. 71).

Chance 4 "is the kind of luck that develops during a probing action that has a distinctive personal flavor" (1978, p. 75). Chance 4 involves behavior focused in a specific manner that results from the investigator's own unique combination of skills, interests, background, aptitudes, personality, values, and beliefs, that is, from the person the investigator is. Chance 3 involves personal sensory receptivity; chance 4, personalized motor behavior (action); chance 2, generalized motor activity. Austin (1978) presents examples of all four types.

The results of chance are not all beneficial in research; they can also be harmful. It is easier to be aware of beneficial results of the intervention of chance than it is to be aware of the negative results. We can understand what someone means who says, "I stumbled across a solution yesterday." To be aware of negative effects of chance is an internal contradiction. It is like saying, "I would know the answer if bad luck hadn't kept me from finding it yesterday." It is easy to see, however, that chances 3 and 4 have harmful as well as helpful results.

The existence of Murphy's Law and its correlatives and variations are evidence of the awareness of the negative effects of chance. Austin (1978, pp. 95, 96) presents twenty such laws. The simplest version of Murphy's Law is: If anything *can* go wrong, it will." Another version is: If anything seems to be going well, you have obviously overlooked something. Then we have the Compensation Corollary: The experiment may be considered a success if no more than fifty percent of your observed results must be discarded to obtain a correlation with your hypothesis.

A person has some control over luck. One of the brightest and most ingenious graduate students I ever worked with, who went on to a successful career in research and administration, told me, "With my luck I don't need brains." Of course what he was overlooking was the fact that if he had been less bright and less ingenious and had exercised less initiative and persistence, he would not have been so lucky. To a substantial extent he made his own good luck. This is true for all of us. We cannot determine our luck but we can influence it, just as we can influence our unconscious minds. Possession of a lively curiosity, active imagination, acute perception, retentive memory, ability to find unexpected similarities, and persistence will do a great deal to improve your luck.

We experience the fortunate results of serendipity when we discover that a method used to solve one problem is appropriate for solving a second problem that was not previously perceived as having any relation to the first or that a solution to one problem turns out to be a solution to an apparently unrelated problem. Serendipity happens often enough to justify Polya's advice (1957, p. 65): "Having made some discovery, however modest, . . . we should not miss the possibilities opened up by the new result, we should try to use again the procedure used. Exploit your success! *Can you use the result, or the method, for some other problem?*"

Polya's suggestion is to look for problems to fit your solution or method. Try to imagine various ways that the solved problem could be described. Consider the ways it is like other situations in addition to how it differs from them. This search activity is a valuable intellectual capital investment. It can provide you with solutions to other problems that you have previously been unable to solve. It can even convert what will otherwise be a difficult challenge when encountered next year into a simple job. In the search, look at parts as well as wholes because a part of the present solution may be all that is needed to solve another problem.

In retrospect, I can see that some of my most productive hours have been spent in doing what Polya advises: tracing out consequences of something I had recently discovered, even though they led far afield from the problem on which I was working when I made the discovery, and even though they related to problems I had no intention of studying at the time and curiosity was my only reason for trying to investigate them. Tracing out the unforeseen consequences of my recent discovery led to implications that I was able to use later (sometimes years later) in studying problems that I would have been unable to formulate or solve had I not done so.

How many of the unsolved problems we face in economic research may actually have been solved, but no one is aware of it because a researcher stumbled upon the solution without realizing it while concentrating on another problem? It can happen that a satisfactory solution to the problem a person is working on is provided by an idea that had been an unsatisfactory solution to a previous problem. Thus we might ask Polya's question not only about results or methods that solve the problem they were intended to solve but also about results or methods that fail to solve the problem for which they were intended. The latter may solve other equally significant problems.

An example is found in the history of alligation, which was taught in arithmetic courses at least as far back as 1809 and seems to have been dropped from arithmetic books around 1900. The purpose of alligation was to find a mixture of several ingredients that would have a specified average quality. Alligation found, in linear programming terms, basic feasible solutions but not necessarily basic optimal feasible solutions. Waugh (1958, p. 94) wrote of two arithmetic texts that discussed alligation (one published in 1809 and one in 1880):

Neither of them discusses the practical problem of mixing three ingredients in such a way as to meet two specifications — to say nothing of the general problem of mixing n ingredients to meet $n - 1$ specifications. This seems rather surprising because it requires only a slight extension of the principles of alligation and our ancestors must have had many practical problems involving several specifications. Anyway we have such problems today. We call them linear programming problems.

Alligation was a forerunner of linear programming. It is interesting to speculate on the history of economics since 1900 or even since the early 1800s if the possibilities of alligation had been recognized and exploited and had led to the earlier development of linear programming. After all, Lovacs (1980, p. 141) has observed, "It is surprising that such a natural and elementary problem as, say, that of finding a solution of [linear programming constraints] was not found two or three centuries ago." His statement, of course, is a manifestation of the fact that many things are obvious after someone points them out.

Following Polya's advice will make for a more productive career in research. It will make workers actually more productive while making them apparently luckier. The success will not, however, represent good luck; it will be the fruit of systematic application of Polya's advice.

Polya's suggestions would worry some economists. These people have expressed a concern that "too many economists are method-oriented rather than rather than problem-oriented. They learn a method and then search around for problems to try it on." I think Polya's proposal is justified, and their concern is justified: for different groups of people. Polya's advice is for you if you already know several tools (or models or methods) and have recently learned another. You can (and should) view the new tool from the perspective provided by your knowledge of other tools and the problems to which they have been applied. For any problem to which you might consider applying a new tool, you can compare that tool with others in relation to how well they fit the problem; and can compare the contemplated problem with other problems to which the familiar tools have been applied. Polya's advice is not appropriate for you if you know only one or two methods. If you know only one model or method and try to make every problem fit it or if you search to find problems on which you can use it, you are a danger to yourself, your employer, and your profession. In following Polya's advice we must avoid Box's (1976) cook-bookery or mathematistry. Ackoff (1979, p. 94) has accused the operations research (OR) profession of suicide by cookbookery, of having ended its own usefulness by its slavish devotion to favorite methods. OR "practitioners decreasingly took problematic situations as they came, but increasingly sought, selected, and distorted them so that favoured techniques could be applied to them. This reduced the usefulness of OR, a reduction that was well recognized by executives who pushed it further and further down in their organizations, to where such relatively simple problems arose as permitted the application of OR's mathematically sophisticated but contextually naive techniques." It is certainly possible to avoid cookbookery and mathematistry while following Polya's advice.

In the discussion of tension (Sect. 12), Bale's use of a treasure map to keep his thoughts focused on his desired goal and to strengthen his desire to achieve that goal was discussed. The idea of a treasure map leads to the idea of a treasure tree. While considering ways to reach the treasure on the map, one is likely to have ideas that also lead to other treasures.

21 *Problem solving*

PSYCHOLOGISTS' STUDIES of problem solving are relevant to us in three ways. Integrating Austin's four classes of chance with their findings shows that it is inevitable that outcomes of research are affected by chance and reinforces my assertion in Section 20 that it is up to us to be prepared to convert chance events into lucky events. The psychologists' work explains why it is that an ability to see (or create) new analogies and other similarities promotes creativity. Doing research requires problem solving. "The conscious task before the scientist is always the solution of a problem. . ." (Popper 1962, p. 222). The problem may be one that business people face daily. It may originate in a scientist's need to satisfy his or her own curiosity about a poorly understood phenomenon. Psychologists' findings provide some insight into tackling the problems that arise in research. They also amplify and justify some of the things written earlier, especially in Section 11 under Have you seen similar problems?, Does a model fit?, and Use reiteration.

Up to this point I have used the term "problem" in the everyday dictionary meaning, that is, a question proposed for solution, hence a perplexing question, situation, or person. From now on I will follow Raaheim (1974) and use "problem" in the narrower technical sense in which he uses it: a problem is one kind of task. What I discussed as "problem formulation" under Thorough preparation in Section 11 becomes "task formulation" under the new definition.

Three Tasks. Raaheim differentiates among three kinds of tasks. He first conceives of a series of earlier situations. A problem situation is "the deviant member of a series of earlier situations of the same sort" (1974, p. 22). The definition focuses at once on the elements that are common to the problem situation and the earlier situations as well as the difference between them. Three aspects of the concept are especially relevant to our discussion (1974, p. 24):

1. "For any particular situation S_i, there is always a great number of *sorts of situations* such that for each of them S_i is a situation of that sort. . . ."
2. "For any given problem situation S_n, there are as many different such series as there are different ways of conceiving what is the deviation in S_n."
3. "At the moment of being confronted with a problem situation, a person may *reclassify* some elements of . . . past experience, and for the first time bring together this and that situation from the past as being of the same sort. . . ."

This definition treats as problems those "tasks which may eventually be solved by *intelligently* utilizing one's past experience" (1974, p. 50) because intelligent behavior depends on an ability to reformulate one's past experience to meet the requirements of the present.

A second kind of task is a routine task, which is not detectably different from previous situations of the same sort. Handling such tasks does not require application of intelligence but use of memory. The third kind is a novel task in which "the deviation from what are the familiar features is too great . . . when a familiar pattern is no longer recognizable" (1974, p. 83).

This categorization also implicitly focuses on the characteristics and experiences of the decision maker involved. For example, academic economists and business people face different sets of tasks. The same decision situation that presents business people with a problem because it deviates somewhat from a series of earlier, similar situations would present academic economists with a novel task because they previously have experienced no such situations.

Intelligence is not a factor in solving novel tasks either. Application of intelligence to such tasks can delay or even prevent finding a solution. "For the effective handling of very unfamiliar tasks, an exploratory activity is more rewarding than intelligent reflection" (1974, p. 84). "With increasing unfamiliarity, the need for active exploration increases, while intelligence seems to play a role of decreasing importance" (1974, p. 89). As Raaheim (1974, p. 92) succinctly states it,

"Being intelligent does not necessarily imply that one has to act intelligently on all occasions!" In science, acutely uncomfortable novel tasks arise when anomalous findings raise serious questions about the validity of an accepted paradigm. As pointed out by Kuhn (1969, p. 87), scientific activities at such times will be of the random, trial-and-error searching type that Raaheim describes. Shideler (1966, p. 122) describes another situation where research consists of fishing expeditions "in search of the characteristics and properties of things under new conditions." Hutchinson (1949, p. 50) asserts that work on really difficult tasks (which almost by definition are the ones that do not yield to your first few efforts) leads eventually, if not initially, to trial-and-error attacks and random activity.

A trial-and-error sequence that starts as a random, blind search may remain that. It may also turn into a cybernetic or feedback process in which a hypothesis is formulated, tried, revised, retested, revised, and so on. If you can determine why an error is an error, you are closer to a solution than before. Identifying the error in a proposed solution tells you something about the nature of your task and it often suggests what needs to be done to make the proposed solution better. And identifying what is not wrong with the solution simplifies your task by telling you things that you need not look for any longer.

The relation between this classification and science education is clear. Kuhn (1969) uses the term "exemplars" to refer to problem solutions that students learn from assignments, examinations, and textbook problems. By solving these, students learn to convert novel tasks into problems and problems into routine tasks.

This categorization also helps us to see one of the benefits of experience. What is a novel task to a novice may only be a problem to an experienced person. And what is a problem to a beginner may be a routine task to an experienced person. Where an experienced person sees a problem, a novice may not see any task at all.

Gestalt psychology emphasizes the desirability of understanding the general principles that underlie specific instances. Raaheim's treatment reinforces the desirability of this understanding. It allows a person to see a particular task as routine because exactly the same general principles that applied to a number of previous tasks also apply to the present one. But a person who lacks the general understanding fails to see how the general principles apply to the specifics of the present task and may even see it as a novel task.

Reclassification. Part of the process of classifying (and defining) the task that you face is the search for identical or similar situations faced earlier. Part of this process will involve redefining or reclassifying earlier situations; part involves defining and classifying the present task. Cognitive psychologists have pointed out that even though a person has all the experience needed to classify the task correctly and to solve it, that person may be unable to bring these past experiences to bear. A person may be able to classify the task correctly and to solve it if it is perceived or presented in one way but may be unable to classify and solve it if perceived or presented in another. It is possible to have in view all the elements needed to solve a task and still be unable to solve it because recognition of the solution requires a bisociation that the subconscious never forms or requires a classification of past experiences or of the present task that is not achieved.

In one of Duncker's experiments on problem solving (described in Koestler 1964, pp. 189–90), each experimental subject was led to a table containing a variety of miscellaneous items including a nail, a cord, and a piece of metal and was told to make a pendulum. The instructions to one group of experimental subjects called the piece of metal a "pendulum weight," and the weight was attached to the cord. Only half of these subjects solved the problem; they used the piece of metal both as a hammer and as a pendulum weight. The second group were of the same age and intelligence as the first. Their instructions did not call the metal piece a "pendulum weight," and the metal and cord were not connected. All these subjects solved the problem. They were able to form a bisociation in which the metal chunk fit into the pendulum matrix and also into the pounding-tool matrix. The students in the first group who failed to solve the problem were unable to fit the weight into the pounding-tool matrix after being told it belonged in the pendulum matrix.

A common recommendation is to consider a task from different angles, viewpoints, orientations, or approaches. To view situations from different angles, to reclassify situations, to perceive them in different ways all require mental flexibility, willingness to perform mental experiments, and commitment to solution rather than to method. Three simple nouns identify mental techniques that are useful in these activities: selection, emphasis, and simplification. You select some elements of a situation as relevant and others as irrelevant. You select some elements to be emphasized and some to be retained but treated as of secondary importance. You simplify by your selection of irrelevant elements, by narrowing the boundaries of your task, by reducing the number of things to be explained. In reclassifying a situation, you change your selection, emphasis, or simplification.

Of course, an individual who has the experience necessary to classify a task and solve it cannot apply the experience if unable to recall it. One reason that knowing something in diverse ways is useful is that it aids recall. It helps you to convert a novel task into a problem or a problem into a routine task. To know anything (whether a task, a method, a model, an equation, or whatever) in a variety of ways also facilitates its reclassification.

Various writers have observed that frequently the best way to solve a task is by indirection. The psychologist Kohler wrote of the "Umweg," a detour that a person may have to take to reach a goal. Littlefield (1978) wrote of "vague thinking" and Koestler and Hadamard of "thinking aside." There is a similarity between all of these and night vision. If you cannot see a faint star (or other object) at night by looking directly at it, focus your eyes slightly to the side of the star and it will be plainly visible. Sometimes it is as though, "I can't answer that question. But I can answer another question. And its answer provides me a way of answering the first question."

Thinking aside or vague thinking, especially about methods, may help to avoid confusing a (unnecessary) means with an (necessary) end. If your job is to cross the river, you may not need to build a bridge.

In discussing the history of the airplane, de Bono (1974) wrote:

The Wright Brothers succeeded in flying because they set out to build an inherently unstable aircraft, and so concentrated on the controls when everyone else was concentrating on stability [p. 9]. The essence of the Wrights' success lay in the full controllability of their machines in pitch, roll and yaw; the Europeans—until they saw Wilbur perform in 1908—treated the airplane as a winged automobile, whose primitive control surfaces were used more for corrective purposes than to initiate control in the air. . . . The Europeans were at first bent on inherent stability, and their controllability was minimal. . . . The Wrights at first deliberately built their machines inherently *unstable*; as they thought this was the only way to make them controllable [p. 36].

The Wright brothers succeeded by defining the problem to be one of "controllability," while others defined the problem to be one of "stability". Bell (1937, pp. 310–11, 323–24, 326) describes how the mathematicians Abel and Jacobi solved long-standing mathematical tasks by redefining them, by looking at them in a novel way.

Take an example from economics. Economists have long dealt with product quality and product differentiation, generally using the mysterious black box treatment: "How do you know they are differentiated products? Just by looking. You can see they are different but similar." It was only after economists quit asking about "product quality" and "product differentiation" and started asking questions about "characteristics" of products that they began to understand quality and product differentiation. A product is a collection of characteristics. Differentiated products contain the same characteristics but in different proportions. Product quality is derived from product characteristics.

Perception. In searching for the series of previous situations from which S_n deviates and in seeking a solution, you are scanning the exterior world and also your own private interior world. In looking for relevant earlier situations, you are examining your own memories and understanding. In studying S_n, you are scanning the exterior world. The interior and the exterior worlds are not independent. What you perceive in the exterior world is governed by the content and organization of your interior mental world. We try to interpret the exterior in terms that we know. We cannot recognize the unknown. What we see is determined less by what is in front of our eyes than by what is behind them.

It is well recognized that your perceptions are affected by your perceptual organizations. Hanson (1958, Ch. 1) provides an intriguing discussion of this point. Johannes Kepler (1571–1630) regarded the sun as fixed and the earth as moving. Tycho Brahe (1546-1601) believed that the earth was fixed and all other celestial bodies revolved around it. Hanson asks, "If they are standing on a hill watching the dawn do they see the same thing in the east?" He argues that they "see different things and yet they see the same thing. That these things can be said depends upon their knowledge, experience, and theories" (p. 18). Also, "There is a sense, then, in which seeing is a 'theory-laden' undertaking. Observation of x is shaped by prior knowledge of x" (p. 19). In addition, observation of x is shaped by prior knowledge of y if x and y are associated in your mind.

The story of the discovery of the planet Neptune provides an illuminating example. Lalande could have discovered Neptune in May of 1795, but he did not believe what he saw on May 8 and 10 of that year. He saw, but he did not notice; and Neptune remained undiscovered for another half century. In 1845–46 Leverrier and Adams independently investigated the perturbations of Uranus. They concluded that they were caused by another, undiscovered, planet and predicted its location. During the summer of 1846 Challis attempted to verify their hypothesis and sighted the planet four times but failed to identify it as a planet. He saw, but he did not notice. It is no coincidence that he distrusted the hypothesis that he was testing. Galle was the first to notice the new planet, on September 23, 1846. The story is reported in Polanyi (1958, pp. 30, 45, 181–82).

For another example, consider Siegel's (1983) report on the baffling global weather patterns of 1982. Beginning in the spring of 1982, data flowing into the U.S. National Oceanographic and Atmospheric Administration (NOAA) (from satellites, buoys, merchant ships, and research vessels) on ocean temperatures, wind directions, and atmospheric pressures in the South Pacific consistently reported unusual weather patterns. Normally, the area off Peru and Ecuador is a region of high pressure, while the western equatorial Pacific is a region of low pressure; the trade winds flow from South America toward Australia and Indonesia. That spring the pattern was reversed. Atmospheric pressure was high in the western Pacific and low in the eastern Pacific. Winds blew from west to east. The warm El Niño ocean current, which normally appears off Peru and Ecuador about Christmas, appeared that spring. Reports of unusual weather patterns continued to flow into NOAA for several months. The data was rejected because the NOAA computer system was programmed to treat data too far from normal as resulting from faulty instruments. As Gene Rasmussen, chief of the diagnostics center of NOAA's Climate Analysis Center, said later, "It was happening, but people just got locked into their theories and models." How often do you suppose that we economists have become locked into our theories and models and failed to notice what existed because they did not tell us that it did exist?

Judson (1980, p. 172) recounts two other examples. One concerns counting of red and white cells in blood samples:

For many years, textbooks that told how to make the counts and interpret them also maintained that if techniques were being followed correctly, two or more samples from the same blood should not vary in cell counts beyond narrow limits, the "maximum allowable discrepancies." And in practice, lab technicians regularly reported counts that kept within the limits. But then three pathologists at the Mayo Clinic, in Minnesota, checked the standard procedures by a more cumbersome but more accurate technique. . . . They counted many series of blood samples and found the discrepancies within series to be greater, at least two-thirds of the time, than the supposed limits. . . . In other words, many observers for many years were making and recording observations that agreed with their expectations but not with the realities.

Another of Judson's examples of "observer effects" is the "discovery" of N rays, a nonexistent type of radiation, in 1903. For examples from economics of effects of expectations (or desires) on observation, see Hutchison's (1981, Ch. 3) summary of M. H. Dobb's writings on Russia and Joan Robinson's on China. For reference to instances in which students of consumer behavior let their wishes determine their perceptions, see Ferber (1979).

Humans (including those who are scientists) have a tendency to see the expected or the desired and to miss the unexpected or undesired even when it is there. One special implication of this is that we need to be sensitive to the unexpected and the contradictory.

There are important differences between task solving in psychological experiments and task solving in real life situations. An analogy with the psychologists' two-string problem can show what I mean. In this problem, each experimental subject is to tie together two strings that hang from a ceiling, but they are so far apart that the subject cannot hold a string in one hand and reach the other. In one version the subject can use any of the following objects to solve the problem: saw, yardstick, awl, pack of nails, screwdriver. In the two-string problem, the experimenter defines the problem and provides items that can be used in its solution. In an examination, the professor defines the problem after providing information you need for its solution. But after you are out of school you are sometimes figuratively given the string, saw, yardstick, and so forth, and asked, What is the task? Sometimes you are given the objects and must ask yourself if a task exists. Sometimes you must search out the items and ask, Is there a task?

If we now define task as, say, "explain an observed phenomenon" or "determine consequences of introduction of unit-train rates for hauling grain" we can see many links between task solving in research and Austin's four kinds of chance.

PART IV

University training for creative scientists

MANY economics graduate students will have academic careers and will face the challenge of preparing a new generation of students for careers of discovery. From the previous sections we can draw some inferences that will help to accomplish this. Although all academics claim to value creativity, I fear that the only creative act that some of us admire is the discovery of new evidence that we were right all the time. We must be prepared to accept the fact that if we train our students well they will discover that we were not always right.

22 Use of exemplars

CREATIVITY can be divided into two stages: obtaining new ideas and evaluating ideas. The development of the critical faculty, it is generally agreed, can be nurtured through education. Most participants at a conference on the creative processes in science and medicine agreed that the creative faculty could be developed through the "master-apprentice relationship that arises from working with a successful scientist" (Maugh 1974). In a master-apprentice relationship, a student learns by active, but limited and guided, self-aware participation in a research or task-solving process. The student learns by doing and observing. But the master-apprentice relationship is not the only way that students' creativity can be developed in a university. Instructors help students to prepare for productive research careers by making proper use of exemplars.

Kuhn (1969, pp. 187–91) discussed paradigms as shared examples:

> By [exemplars] I mean, initially, the concrete problem situations that students encounter from the start of their scientific education; whether in laboratories, on examinations, or at the ends of chapters in science texts . . . [and] at least some of the technical problem-solutions found in the periodical literature that students encounter during their post-educational research careers and that also show them by example how their job is to be done [p. 187].

In working on exemplars, students are learning things about nature and also how to give empirical content to theories and concepts they have studied. As an example, Kuhn (1969, pp. 188–89) discusses Newton's Second Law of Motion, which relates force to mass and acceleration as $f = ma$:

> It is not quite the case that logical and mathematical manipulations are applied directly to $f = ma$. That expression proves on examination to be a law-sketch or law-schema. As the student or the practicing scientist moves from one problem situation to the next, the symbolic generalization to which such

manipulations apply changes. For the case of free fall, $f = ma$ becomes $mg = md^2s/dt^2$; for the simple pendulum it is transformed to $mg \sin \theta = -mld^2\theta/dt^2$; for a pair of interacting harmonic oscillations it becomes two equations, the first of which may be written $m_1d^2s_1/dt^2 + k_1s_1 = k_2 (s_2 - s_1 + d)$; and for more complex situations, such as the gyroscope, it takes still other forms, the family resemblance of which to $f = ma$ is still harder to discover. Yet, while learning to identify forces, masses, and accelerations in a variety of physical situations not previously encountered, the student has also learned to design the appropriate version of $f = ma$ through which to interrelate them, often a version for which he has encountered no literal equivalent before. How has he learned to do this?

Kuhn's answer to this question could have come right from Raaheim: "The student discovers, with or without the assistance of his instructor, a way to see his problem as *like* a problem he has already encountered" (p. 189, emphasis mine). The several variants of $f = ma$ show that the similarity in Raaheim's similar sort of situation may be a similarity only to the well tutored and may require a great deal of perception and imagination to identify.

This last quotation from Kuhn contains an important insight into the training of students for careers as creative scientists. Kuhn wrote, "the student *discovers*" (emphasis mine), not the student is taught, or is told, but discovers. His felicitous expression presents a fundamental insight. A student must discover answers that are already known in order to develop into a scientist who discovers answers that are not now known. Students can learn to discover only by practicing discovery.

A number of people have written on the importance of learning by discovering. "Between the work of the student who tries to solve a problem in geometry or algebra [or economics] and a work of invention, one can say that there is only a difference of degree, a difference of level, both works being of a similar nature" (Hadamard 1954, p. 104). Discovery-learning is learning by doing.

Poincare (1913, p. 385) wrote, "It seems to me then in repeating a lesson learned, that I could have invented it. This is often only an illusion, but even then, even if I am not so gifted as to create it by myself, I myself re-invent it in so far as I repeat it." Piaget wrote (1973, p. 20), "To understand is to discover, or reconstruct by rediscovery. . . ." Also, "The goal of intellectual education is . . . in learning to master the truth by oneself at the risk of losing a lot of time and of going through all the roundabout ways that are inherent in real activity" (p. 106).

Various people have observed that discovery is its own reward. In discovery-learning the student does get to experience the excitement of discovery. As Koestler (1975, p. 266) puts it, "Confronting the student . . . with the finished solution means depriving him of all excitement, to shut off the creative impulse, to reduce the adventure of mankind to a dusty heap of theorems."

By their participation in discovery-learning, students learn the necessity of taking risks in solving problems and novel tasks. If the exemplars are properly selected, the students will have to try some approaches they have not tried before, to venture new (to them) ideas, to develop new arguments. They find that many tasks cannot be solved by mechanical application of the already known but require novel application of what is known.

Ph.D. dissertations are exercises in discovery-learning in which the teacher does not know the answer either. Term paper assignments and group projects can also be exercises in exploring the unknown.

Torrance and Myers (1970) mention two of the values of discovery-learning: "Facts and ideas may be dismissed, forgotten, or discredited; but it is difficult to dismiss, forget, or discredit an experience—a truly personal contact with a fact or idea" (p. 6). Experiencing a solution provides deeper and more enduring understanding than reading a solution. "You cannot dismiss [experiences] as you can facts. They become a part of you . . . because they engage the intellect, the emotions, the spirit, and generate feelings and attitudes" (p. 16).

Torrance and Myers (1970, pp. 310–13) present students' ideal teacher checklist results. Among university students the most desirable teacher characteristic (out of 66) was "encourages me to think." Discovery-learning provides students something they value (encouragement to think) and also provides something of value to them when they are no longer students (enduring understanding).

Synge (1951, pp. 19–33) has presented a little game he calls VISH (for vicious circles), which metaphorically demonstrates the value of teaching by exemplars. For example, to learn the definition of "point," you find in the dictionary, point = that which has position but not magnitude. Next, magnitude = size. Next, size = magnitude. And, magnitude = size. What does this circle show? That the definition of point is logically inadequate. To understand its meaning requires knowing the meaning of magnitude, which requires knowing the meaning of size, which requires. . . . Just like cycling in a degenerate linear program! This is a four-step case of VISH. Other cases require many more steps. But the issue is a pervasive one because every word is defined in a dictionary or textbook by other words. If you do not already know the meanings of all the other words, you will have to look them up and if they are defined in terms of other un-known words, you will have to look *them* up too. You will ultimately come across a word with unknown meaning that you have already encountered. At this point you have won the game; you have a VISH.

Precisely because dictionaries use words to define words, we can-not learn the meanings of *all* words from dictionaries. Before we can make profitable use of a dictionary we must know the meanings of *some* words. How do we learn these? We learn them by experiencing them. Working on exemplars accomplishes this; it takes a widely diverse group of people and subjects them to shared experiences. They learn meanings by experiencing meanings. By requiring students to share experiences, among themselves and with us as teachers, we as-sure a common vocabulary.

One becomes powerfully aware of the importance of the shared experiences of exemplars in providing common meanings when one tries to do interdisciplinary work. For example, I had spent many hours spread over a period of more than a year studying animal breed-ing textbooks and lecture notes and talking with animal breeders, and I understood their textbook definitions. I soon came to realize that they all spoke to me as they would to sophomore students in introduc-tory classes, thus I understood them. But when I listened to them talk among themselves, I was confused most of the time, while they all made perfect sense of what they said to each other. On the other hand, even after they had studied economics diligently and lengthily, I was unable to convey to them ideas that were easily understood by fellow economists. The longer the animal breeders and I worked to-gether, the easier it became for us to communicate. But there always remained that perceptible residue of the uncommunicable. It re-mained because we had relatively few shared experiences. If I had taken some of their laboratory and field experience courses and worked on their exemplars, and they had taken economics courses and worked on economics exemplars, we would have sharply reduced the size of that residue of the uncommunicable.

Note also Kuhn's phrase "with or without the instructor's assist-ance." How can instructors assist students to discover? We cannot help them to learn to discover if we always tell them what is to be discovered or how to discover it. Polya's work on heuristic reasoning (1954a, 1954b, 1957) contains a number of valuable suggestions for teachers who want to turn out creative scientists. Heuristic concerns methods and rules of discovery and invention. Polya (1957) presents and explains the use of a list of cue questions that instructors can address to students (and scientists can address to themselves) to facilitate their discovery of correct answers. My list of questions in Section 11 was stimulated by Polya's work, and some of my questions are virtually the same as his.

Kuhn discusses exemplars in the context of physical sciences. Let us look at an example in economics: applications of linear programming to learn the meaning of "activity." A typical definition of activity reads, "An activity is characterized by the flow over time of items into or out of the activity, or both. One purpose of linear programming is to determine the activity levels required to accomplish a given objective. The level of the jth activity is a continuous variable, frequently represented by x_j. The jth activity is represented by a set of coefficients, frequently represented by a_{ij}, where a_{ij} equals the time rate of flow of the ith item into or out of the jth process per unit level of that process. For each process j, the ratio a_{ij}/a_{hj} is constant for all i and h." Even though you know the meaning of every symbol (remember, words are symbols) in that quotation and even though you are literate in the English language, if you have not worked with linear (or quadratic) programming, you do not know the meaning and use of "activity" if that definition is all you know about it. To help students to learn the meaning, actually the meanings, an instructor will present exemplars in class and have the students work on others in tests or homework assignments. If students make enough different applications of linear programming, they will discover that the quoted definition must be stretched considerably to make it describe the activities in some programs and will also see that the definition cannot be stretched or transformed in any way to make it conform to some things treated as activities.

Even for a person who has never had any experience on a farm or in a machine shop, it is straightforward to see the connection between the definition of activity and various ways of producing different things and describing the ways by using column vectors that represent activities. The connections are also reasonably straightforward in diet and blending problems. But how would a person ever get from the definition of activity to the use of programming as a statistical estimation procedure? If programming is used to estimate a consumer demand function, say, each activity is represented by a vector of the sample values of one variable and the level of the activity is the value of the variable's coefficient.

As one can easily infer from this example, knowing a definition too well and believing it too thoroughly can be a deterrent to task solving. There does not seem to be any way to make the definition of "activity" fit the description "sample values of consumer income", say, and make the definition of "level of activity" fit "coefficient of consumer income." If you insist on a clear connection between your programming variables and the verbal textbook definition of activity level, you will overlook some applications of programming.

It occurs to me that this example and Kuhn's discussion of $f = ma$ provide additional evidence in support of Warnock's position that we need imagination to join concepts to sense experience (Sect. 17).

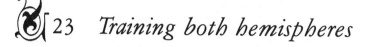

23 *Training both hemispheres*

THE EARLIER MATERIAL on hemispheral lateralization (Sect. 4) leads to several inferences on training and helps us to see additional values of using exemplars. One inference is that our current educational system with its emphasis on verbalization and analysis addresses itself primarily to training the LH. Emphasis on verbalization prevents students from developing a proper appreciation for and skill in imagery, endocept, and tacit knowledge (Polanyi 1958, Chs. 5, 6). Tacit knowledge is acquired through experience and is not, and perhaps cannot be, articulated. But it does influence behavior. By using exemplars, we help students to develop their own tacit knowledge, and possibly we even pass on some of our own as students learn by observing what we do. Of course, the instructor's lectures on exemplars provide necessary LH training. Some problems can be solved by either analysis or synthesis. Some require both. Students who are taught only one method are handicapped in attacking tasks for which the other is more effective or both are required. Emphasizing verbalization and analysis discriminates against the student whose RH is dominant. In discovery-learning, the student can use either one, whichever is more comfortable, and many exemplars require using both.

Some experimental results indicate that inductive learning is as effective or more so than deductive learning for RH-dominant students, whereas deductive learning is more effective for the LH dominant. Inductive learning involves synthesizing wholes from parts, whereas deductive learning proceeds from rules to examples. The earlier discussion would lead us to expect these results because the RH is superior for synthesis, the LH for analysis. Learning by discovery provides deductive and inductive experiences. Williams (1983) presents techniques for training ourselves and students to utilize RH processes in learning and task solving.

We write of hemispheric dominance, not of hemispheric monopoly. Regardless of which hemisphere (if either) is dominant, both need training. Teaching methods such as laboratory exercises, homework assignments, and field experience encourage greater RH participation in learning. We cannot control the psychological makeup of our students. The best we can do is to use a variety of teaching methods so that we train both hemispheres of LH- and RH-dominated students.

And finally, although there is little that we as university instructors can do to solve the problem by ourselves, we must observe that training, even excellent training, in the three Rs is not adequate for science or for life. The three Rs are all LH processes. Unless the students can rise above their education, instruction limited to the three Rs produces spiritually impoverished citizens and unproductive scientists.

24 Exposing students to the unknown

A NUMBER of people who have studied the teaching of creativity have concluded that it is desirable to expose students to our ignorance as well as our knowledge. Taylor (1966, p. 57) writes, "More time should be allowed during instruction and more attention in all instructional materials to what we *do not know* and how one might generally get started to find the answers to things not currently known." Torrance (1966, p. 162) and Beck (1966, p. 221) write of the desirability of having textbooks that present knowledge as incomplete (with gaps, unknowns, anomalies, and uncertainties) and of having instructional materials that show the state of knowledge at the frontier of a discipline. Taylor (1966, p. 16) approvingly mentions a college-level elementary physics text in which the author included puzzles to which no one knew the answers in order to start students thinking about them. Twenty-five years after the event, Austin (1978, pp. 4–5) clearly recalled the excitement that he and fellow medical students in a neurology class felt when their teachers forcefully debated the proper diagnosis of a patient's disease. It was a heady experience to be exposed to controversy and gaps in their information and to realize that there was still useful knowledge to be discovered. Presenting questions we cannot answer demonstrates to students that it is respectable, even desirable, to have doubts and raise questions. Teaching that some unknowns are worth knowing and some gaps are worth filling shows students that it is possible to acquire something valuable by venturing into the unknown.

In Torrance and Myers's ideal teacher checklist of 66 items (1970, pp. 310–13), "is open-minded" and "respects my ideas" were ranked eleventh by university students. Students value teachers with inquiring minds who give students' ideas a fair hearing. University students' fourth most desirable teacher characteristic was "causes me to be curious." I can think of no better way to excite students' curiosity than by exposing them to teasing and challenging questions, gaps, and uncertainties and suggesting to them the possibility of marvelous, clever, and elegant discoveries that they may contribute to science. The eighth most desirable teacher characteristic in the list was "is excited about learning." Where does an instructor's excitement about learning come from? By far the major excitement comes from new discovery: from learning something no one has known before. If this is an instructor's major source of excitement, he or she should share it with students to let them enjoy the excitement also. One way an instructor can accomplish this is by sharing the opportunities for new discovery with students. Torrance and Myers (1972, pp. 54–55) suggest a number of strategies for using incompleteness of knowledge to motivate student achievement.

Some topics that I have taught for some time, know well, and have well-organized notes on are much less exciting to the students now than they were several years ago when I knew little about them but was actively doing research on them and regularly coming up with new questions and new answers. Looking back at my working papers reminds me of the crudity and inadequacy of the questions and answers I had then. But the students taking the course at that time seemed to experience a vicarious thrill of discovery that the present students do not. Perhaps a more accurate title for this section would be, "Teaching the almost unknown and the barely known."

There is an additional argument for covering what we do not know. We are trying to prepare students to face the next thirty, forty, or fifty years. The methods we teach today may be inadequate or irrelevant in ten years. One skill that we can help students develop, which they will need throughout their careers, is a skill at asking questions.

Students must learn to evaluate ideas as well as to generate them and to separate the two processes, and they ought to learn the art of creative evaluation. Creative evaluation tries to spot weaknesses and cure them, whereas critical evaluation simply exposes them. The former looks for constructive possibilities; the latter, merely for defects. Appreciating the distinction is important because it is easy to criticize but it is more difficult to be right. Instructors can help students to learn creative evaluation while working on discovery-learning of exemplars and on gaps and unknowns.

In relation to covering the unknown, there is another thing we can do. It is enough to have students uncertain about a new solution to an old problem or a new solution to a new problem. We should avoid giving additional causes for uncertainty. Students need to know that failure will not lead to ridicule or loss of respect from professors; that criticism of their efforts is not criticism of them; that they are respected and valued, though junior, colleagues; that they are expected to contribute ideas; that their contributions will be received in the scientific spirit in which they are offered and will receive serious, professional evaluation from you; that you expect them to carefully evaluate your ideas as well as their own and to report their evaluations frankly; that their creativity is encouraged. (I have published a number of mistakes in my career. I might have published even more if my students had not corrected them.) In brief, we need to provide students an environment in which they can (and are encouraged and expected to) experiment, take risks, be uncertain, fail, and succeed. It is hard to try anything if you have to worry about being slapped down if you fail. Furthermore, if you know that you will be slapped down for trying, you soon lose your desire to try. But if you know that it is safe to try and you will be rewarded for succeeding, you will be motivated to proceed. Students need to know that their inventiveness is valued by their professors. Note (the point made earlier in the book), it is inventiveness, not mere novelty, that is valued.

25 *Self-discipline*

WE MUST HELP students to appreciate the importance of self-discipline, which is needed for the hard work of thorough preparation. Without it students will succumb to the temptation to begin working on problems before they are ready. It is needed for the conscious effort of complete verification. Without it the student will accept a wrong, but beautiful, solution after partial testing. Exploitation requires self-discipline and patience. It requires self-discipline to take the time necessary to prepare a report of your results when you have lost interest in the original problem and are impatient to start work on another. It takes self-discipline to temporarily abandon a problem that you feel a compulsion to finish or a question that hurts because you are so anxious to know the answer. Self-discipline is required to prevent environmental influences from becoming distractions; to provide the flexible persistence that keeps you coming back to a problem even when temporarily discouraged; to set priorities that allow you time for speculating, intuiting, or daydreaming; to prevent the conscious mind from applying its critical standards to inhibit the free flow of thoughts while speculating.

Many graduate students already know self-discipline. For the ones who do not discipline themselves, perhaps all that we professors can do is to keep their noses to the grindstone until they decide that self-discipline is preferable to a professor's discipline. Arieti (1976, pp. 378–79) lists discipline as a necessary condition for creativity.

One responsibility of a teacher is to motivate students to want to learn the things that the teacher believes are important. Teachers sometimes fail to meet this responsibility. Then students need the self-discipline to learn while indifferent to what they are learning.

In self-initiated learning, the teacher does not face the problem of motivating students. Students are motivated by their own curiosity. Drevdahl (1964, p. 178) wrote that "a nondirective, relatively unstructured advanced training is of significant benefit. The outstanding feature, educationally, is that the creative group and to some extent the noncreative productive group, received what might be described as a 'laissez-faire' type of graduate training." The creative group and the noncreative productive group of students had few required courses; research was encouraged even at the expense of formal courses; they had substantial freedom of choice in selecting courses and research. Other students of the teaching of creativity who have found benefits in a laissez-faire type training are Taylor (1966, p. 6) and Torrance (1962, pp. 11–12, 145). I suspect that one reason that a laissez-faire philosophy of education trains creative researchers is that it provides students a broader training and more diverse experiences than a more directed education.

26 *Deliberate creative task solving*

SOME SYSTEMATIC METHODS of creative task solving have been developed for use by groups. Two of these are called "creative problem solving" (Osborn 1963; Parnes et al. 1977) and "synectics" (Prince 1970; Gordon et al. 1961; Gordon and Poze 1980) by their developers. (Note that I continue to use task and problem in the Raaheim sense, although Osborn and Parnes do not use them in this sense.) In essence, these are systematic methods that groups can use to apply ideas in this essay to each of the steps of the inventive process. Any seminar, workshop, or committee that wants to tackle unresolved issues may make fruitful use of these methods. Of course, any system has a better chance of success if members want a solution and are motivated; are sufficiently comfortable with themselves and the others to risk voicing half-baked, innovative ideas; are free from distractions; and are free from the urge to protect their turf or dominate the show.

The creative problem solving process consists of five steps:

1. Becoming aware of a task.

2. Defining the task. Group members differ in their knowledge, skills, interests, experiences, expectations, and perceptual organization. Consequently, it is to be expected that different members will formulate the task differently. It is not necessary and usually not desirable to get everyone to agree on the same formulation.

3. Producing alternative solutions. This step follows four rules of group brainstorming: (a) The goal is to generate a large number of ideas. (b) This step is reserved for creative thought. Criticism is ruled out. Critical thinking is postponed until the fourth step. (c) All ideas are welcome. (d) Improved ideas and combinations of ideas are sought. The use of metaphor, analogy, and free thinking is encouraged.

4. Evaluating ideas generated in step 3 to select the most promising ones. This requires development of evaluative standards, which may be a significant creative challenge in itself.

5. Making promising ideas acceptable. This may call for additional work to modify the solution, to make it attractive, or to secure its adoption.

27 *Creative teaching*

BEFORE LEAVING the topic of teaching creativity, we should spend some time on creative teaching. Torrance and Myers (1970, p. 3) write, "By the very nature of their roles teachers have to behave in ways characteristic of the creative person." They must be aware and sensitive to developments in the classroom and to needs of students. They must be flexible in order to cope constructively with the unforeseen. They must be spontaneous so they can react quickly and confidently. They must be original to meet the great variety of conditions and incidents encountered. They must be intuitive because they frequently lack time for careful study.

The idea that the excellent teacher is an artist is evidenced by Torrance and Myers (1970, p. 192): "The fascinating and frustrating part of trying to discover just what makes a teacher the kind of person who inspires children to be truly excited about expressing their ideas is that teacher behavior cannot really be reduced to an analysis of either verbal or nonverbal elements. Many intangibles operate to make teachers effective, ineffectual or harmful." The importance of intangibles implies that it will be a long time before we can rely on science to provide the information needed to train good teachers.

Class lectures need frequent revision when discoveries are reported frequently. It is true of myself, and of some others whom I have observed, that periodic revisions are required even if no significant discoveries have been reported for some time. We need to discover new exemplars, devise a new organization, develop a different emphasis, or find a new synthesis to regenerate our own interest in a topic and keep our lectures from degenerating into recitations of well-memorized script.

It is possible to be a creative economics teacher without being a creative economics researcher and vice versa. Being the former involves such things as imaginative use of exemplars or development of new ones, relating class topics to the current economic situation, and finding analogies and metaphors to help students tie their new knowledge to what they already know.

Section 25 mentions the teacher's responsibility to motivate students. Motivation provides opportunity for an instructor's creativity. One type of motivation convinces students a subject is worth studying. It addresses such questions as, "I already know ordinary least squares and you tell me it is best linear unbiased efficient. Why should I have to learn an additional method?" A second type addresses such issues as, "Before I learn autoregressive least squares, give me an intuitive or heuristic argument to show me that the assumptions and procedure will allow me to handle the problem of autocorrelated errors." My impression is that the need for instructors to motivate graduate students, especially first-year graduate students, has become greater as economics has become more mathematical. Students increasingly wonder why they should spend so much time studying mathematics when they want to become economists.

Creative teaching is not synonymous with teaching creativity, though it is hard to see how we can have imitative teaching of creativity. But I can easily imagine creative teaching of imitativity. I am sure that the psychologists can tell us about various creative methods for suppressing students' curiosity and indoctrinating them to love the current conventional wisdom and to fear and hate new ideas. Do you suppose that it is possible that psychologists could learn some other ingenious methods for suppressing creativity if they visited some economics classrooms?

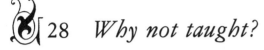

28 *Why not taught?*

THIS SECTION is an example of simple retroduction: retroduction, because we are trying to explain an observed phenomenon; simple, because the explanations will make little use of deductive logic.

Section 2 implied some of the answers to the question, Why do we not devote more attention to training students' unconscious mental processes and developing their inventiveness? Another practical reason is lack of instructors' time. Teachers all know how much easier and quicker it is to grade a conventional examination answer (whether conventionally right or conventionally wrong) than it is to grade an unconventional answer. Not only is extra time required to identify right and wrong parts of an unconventional answer, it is more difficult to fit an unusual error than a common error into a fair grading scheme. One novel answer can require as much time to grade as five conventional answers. Thus grading twelve answers can take twice as long as grading ten. And it is not only at examination time that the imaginative student consumes more of our time.

Do we professors have time to devote attention to stimulating creativity? We do have time to do this when we are working one-on-one with a student who is writing a thesis. I frequently worry that this is too late, that a student who reaches the Ph.D. thesis stage in our present educational system has retained only the residual inventiveness and curiosity that we have not managed to crush out and grind off during the student's previous years in school.

We can do various things in classrooms, though (before students reach the thesis stage), to stimulate students' creativity. We can have speculative and probing classroom discussions and ungraded assignments of questions whose answers are not known as well as discussions and ungraded assignments on questions whose answers are known but not found in lectures or textbooks. Torrance and Myers (1970) devote Chapter 8 to use of provocative questions in classrooms. They discuss interpretation questions, comparison questions, synthetic questions, redefinition questions, evaluation questions, and hypothetical questions. Their book is addressed to public school teachers, and consequently, most of their examples are not appropriate for college level teachers. But their principles are. However, making such assignments and asking provocative questions is not sufficient. They can serve to encourage or discourage creativity, depending upon the instructor's demeanor and attitude.

A number of authors have argued that the fundamental reason for not teaching unconscious thinking and creativity is that the people who set goals for public education do not want them taught. Ackoff (1978, pp. 4–5) writes:

> Most of the affluent do not want to transform society or its parts. They would rather sacrifice what future social progress creative minds might bring about rather than run the risk of losing the products of previous progress that less creative minds are managing to preserve. The principal beneficiaries of contemporary society do not want to risk the loss of the benefits they now enjoy. Therefore, they, and the educational institutions they control, suppress creativity before children acquire the competence that, together with creativity, would enable them to bring about radical social transformations. Most adults fear that the current form and functioning of our society, its institutions, and the organizations within it could not survive the simultaneous onslaught of youthful creativity and competence. Student behavior in the 1960s convinced them of this. . . . The creativity of children is suppressed at home and at school. . . . Schools want [children] to think the way parents want them to think: conservatively, not creatively.

Consequently, while part of the educational process has been devoted to making the science student a good scientist, another part is designed to keep him or her from becoming too good.

Toynbee (1964) expressed a similar idea: "There are two present-day adverse forces that are conspicuously deadly to creativity. One of these is an excessive anxiety to conserve vested interest in acquired wealth" (p. 4). "In present-day America, so it looks to me, the affluent majority is striving desperately to arrest the irresistible tide of change. It is attempting this impossible task because it is bent on conserving the social and economic system under which this comfortable affluence has been acquired" (p. 8).

Recent congressional behavior provides empirical support for the Ackoff-Toynbee view (Harl 1983, p. 850):

> The Congress in 1981 enacted a research credit deductible against calculated income tax for expenditures by firms for basic and applied research. . . . The

credit, at a 25 percent level for research expenditures, subsidizes 25 percent of the cost for research where the present value of the remaining 75 percent is sufficiently greater than zero to compete effectively with alternative investments by the firm. Interestingly, the social sciences are statutorily barred from eligibility for such demand-driven research funding.

If you encourage and teach people to ask questions, they may begin to ask "dangerous" questions. This leads me to another hypothesis. Some who feel threatened by a discovery are teachers. Recognition of the discovery requires accepting the painful fact that part of one's hard-earned knowledge is wrong and some painfully developed skills are obsolete. "What will my colleagues and my recent graduates think of me when they discover that what I have been teaching and using in my research is wrong?"

Another explanation may be found in the false perception that intuition and science are mutually incompatible. I hypothesize that many holders of this view also mistakenly equate scientific method with testing. These people may have misread Popper or misread writings about him. They are aware of his *Logic of Scientific Discovery* (1959), which does not deal with discovery as much as with testing. Most economists seem to have some knowledge of this book, but few seem to be aware of his later *Conjectures and Refutations* (1962) (and I here emphasize the "conjectures"), where he discusses the "hypothetico-inductive method." He argues that scientific knowledge progresses by a cybernetic or feedback process in which we guess or conjecture tentative solutions to problems. The conjectures are tested by attempted refutations, then modified and retested. The method is summarized by Wiener (1956, p. 72):

(1) The imagination of a theory to fit the facts; (2) the deduction of the consequences of the theory; (3) the verification of these consequences and the observation of their errors; (4) the imagination of a theory to account for the errors of the original theory or the formulation of a new theory avoiding these errors. The process runs through a regular never-ending cycle.

The unconscious, the imagination, serves as a source of conjectures, of guesses whose inferences are deduced and subjected (ideally but too infrequently) to stiff testing. Medawar (1969, pp. 42–59) provides a good brief discussion of the hypothetico-deductive method.

The rules of testing, logic, mathematics, and evidence that we rely on so heavily (did you ever ask, Where do they come from? How do we know that they are valid?) are built on logic and experience.

But the foundations of the entire structure are intuition and faith. We can exemplify the truth of this assertion by demonstrating that, for example, our rules of logic originate in unproven propositions. By unproven I mean logically unproven; the propositions have not been logically proven by deriving them as valid implications of a prior set of assumptions.

Suppose that I demonstrate to our complete satisfaction that an economic argument satisfies all the present rules of logical validity. But the argument may still contain error because of errors or contradictions in our rules of logic. So we must develop a super logic to justify our rules of logic. The logical consequences (theorems) of our super logic will be the axioms or assumptions of logic. But our deductive argument may still contain error because our super logic contains error. So we need a super super logic to justify our super logic. The super super logic may be in error. So the next necessary step is a super super super logic . . . and so on and so on. No one has yet followed this regress through many layers of supers. Thus we can say that our rules of logic are based on unproven propositions: the axioms of the last super level developed. These axioms, then, are not the product of deductive effort. They were created by an act of imagination or intuition and are accepted by an act of faith. That this is so is not surprising in light of the fact that the purpose of symbolic logic is to provide a "precise definition of an intuitive notion of logical correctness" (Rosser 1953, p. 8).

We can carry out a similar argument (leading to the same conclusions) for rules of testing. If we apply a similar method of argument to any of our economic theories, we find their foundation, too, in unproven propositions, variously called axioms, postulates, or assumptions. Thus we conclude that the foundations of our science are unknown propositions or unproven propositions. We have a beautiful scientific cathedral built upon a foundation of ghosts.

Popper (1962, p. 20) expressed the same idea this way: "Ideas that are statements or judgments or propositions may be expressed by assertions which may be true and their truth may be reduced, by way of derivations, to that of primitive propositions; the attempt, incidentally, to establish rather than to reduce their truth by these means leads to an infinite regress." And he observes (p. 23) that the attempt to trace all knowledge to its ultimate source in observation also leads to infinite regress.

Synge (1951, esp. pp. 19–34) shows that geometrical reasoning must start with undefined elements and relations and unproven propositions. Trying to define all elements and relations or to prove all propositions leads to vicious circles, to VISHs. The axioms of axiomatic mathematics (the unproven propositions) are creations of imagination.

Polanyi (1958, pp. 184–93) argues that our acceptance of mathematics is based on intuitive and aesthetic standards.

We find, then, that science and imagination are not incompatible. Quite the contrary. Imagination, hunch, and intuition are necessary for science. Without imagination we could not connect concepts and experience. See the discussion of Warnock's (1976) position in Section 17. We need imagination to provide the insights leading to theories that fit the facts. And we rely on intuition for the postulates that support our rules of logic.

References

Ackoff, Russell L. 1978. *The Art of Problem Solving.* New York: Wiley.
————. 1979. The future of operational research is past. *J. Oper. Res. Soc.* 30:93–104.
Allendoerfer, Carl B. 1962. The narrow mathematician. *Am. Math. Monthly* 69(6):461–69.
American Economic Association. 1985. Evsey D. Domar, Distinguished Fellow, 1984. *Am. Econ. Rev.* 75:289.
Arieti, Silvano. 1976. *Creativity: The Magic Synthesis.* New York: Basic Books.
Aronson, Elliott. 1981. Research in social psychology as a leap of faith. In Elliott Aronson, ed., *Readings about the Social Animal,* 3rd ed., Ch. 1. San Francisco: Freeman. Repr. from *Pers. Soc. Psych. Bull.* 3(1977):190–95.
Austin, James H. 1978. *Chase, Chance, and Creativity: The Lucky Art of Novelty.* New York: Columbia Univ. Press.
Bale, Malcolm. 1979. Personal communication, 22 May.
Baumol, William J. 1985. On method in economics a century earlier. *Am. Econ. Rev.* 75(6):1–12.
Beck, Lester F. 1966. Use of films and television for creative teaching. In Calvin W. Taylor and Frank E. Williams, eds., *Instructional Media and Creativity,* pp. 217–24. New York: Wiley.
Bell, E. T. 1937. *Men of Mathematics.* New York: Simon and Schuster.
Beveridge, W. I. B. 1957. *The Art of Scientific Investigation,* rev. ed. New York: Random House.
Bonini, Charles P. 1963. *Simulation of Information and Decision Systems in the Firm.* Englewood Cliffs, N.J.: Prentice-Hall.
Box, George E. P. 1976. Science and statistics. *J. Am. Stat. Assoc.* 71:791–99.
Box, Joan Fisher. 1980. R. A. Fisher and the design of experiments, 1922–1926. *Am. Stat.* 34:1–7.
Braithwaite, Richard B. 1960. *Scientific Explanation: A Study of the Function of Theory, Probability, and Law in Science.* New York: Harper and Row.
Burke, James. 1978. *Connections.* Boston: Little, Brown.
Clardy, Andrea. 1977. In contemplation of her professional navel. Ames, Iowa, *Daily Tribune,* 19 October, p. 4.
Clark, Ronald W. 1971. *Einstein: The Life and Times.* New York: World.
de Bono, Edward, ed. 1974. *Eureka! An Illustrated History of Inventions from the Wheel to the Computer.* New York: Holt, Rinehart, and Winston.
Drevdahl, John E. 1964. Some developmental and environmental factors in creativity. In Calvin W. Taylor, ed. *Widening Horizons in Creativity,* pp. 170–86. New York: Wiley.

Drucker, Peter. 1970. *Technology, Management, and Society.* New York: Harper and Row.

Duesenberry, J. S., G. Fromm, L. R. Klein, and E. Kuh. 1969. *The Brookings Model: Some Further Results.* Chicago: Rand McNally, Amsterdam: North-Holland.

Ernst, Max. 1952. Inspiration to order. In Brewster Ghiselin, ed. *The Creative Process,* pp. 58–61. Berkeley: Univ. California Press.

Ferber, Robert. 1979. How not to write a prize-winning article. *J. Consum. Res.* 5:303–5.

Ferber, Robert, and P. J. Verdoorn. 1962. *Research Methods in Economics and Business.* New York: Macmillan.

Feynman, Richard (interview). 1983. *NOVA: The Pleasure of Finding Things Out.* Boston: WGBH Educational Foundation.

Foote, Richard J. 1958. *Analytical Tools for Studying Demand and Price Structures.* USDA, Agric. Handb. 146, Washington, D.C.

Fox, Karl A. 1958. *Econometric Analysis for Public Policy.* Ames: Iowa State Univ. Press.

_____. 1974. *Social Indicators and Social Theory: Elements of an Operational System.* New York: Wiley.

_____. 1983. The eco-behavioral view of human societies and its implications for systems science. *Int. J. Sys. Sci.* 14:895–914.

Galbraith, John Kenneth. 1960. *The Liberal Hour.* Boston: Houghton Mifflin.

Gordon, William J. J., and associates. 1961. *Synectics: The Development of Creative Capacity.* New York: Harper and Row.

Gordon, William J. J., and Tony Poze. 1980. *The New Art of the Possible.* Cambridge, Mass.: Porpoise Books.

Guilford, J. P. 1967. Intellectual factors in productive thinking. In Ross L. Mooney and Taher A. Razik, eds., *Explorations in Creativity,* pp. 95–106. New York: Harper and Row.

Hadamard, Jacques. 1954. *The Psychology of Invention in the Mathematical Field.* New York: Dover.

Hansen, Flemming. 1981. Hemispheral lateralization: Implications for understanding consumer behavior. *J. Consum. Res.* 8:23–36.

Hanson, Norwood R. 1958. *Patterns of Discovery.* New York: Cambridge Univ. Press.

Harl, Neil E. 1983. Agricultural economics: Challenges to the profession. *Am. J. Agric. Econ.* 65:845–54.

Hauser, Robert J. 1981. Personal communication, 15 May.

Heilbroner, Robert L. 1983. *The Worldly Philosophers,* 5th rev. ed. New York: Penguin.

Hicks, J. R. 1950. *Value and Capital,* 2nd ed. London: Oxford Univ. Press.

Hilgard, Ernest R., and Gordon H. Bower. 1975. *Theories of Learning,* 4th ed. Englewood Cliffs, N.J.: Prentice-Hall.

Hirshleifer, Jack. 1985. The expanding domain of economics. *Am. Econ. Rev.* 75(6):53–68.

Hofstadter, Douglas R. 1979. *Godel, Escher, Bach: An Eternal Golden Braid.*

New York: Vintage Books.

Hughes, Harold. 1963. Individual and group creativity in science. In M. Coler, ed., *Essays on Creativity in the Sciences,* pp. 93–101. New York: Columbia Univ. Press.

Huizinga, J. 1950. *Homo Ludens: A Study of the Play Element in Culture.* New York: Roy.

Hutchinson, Eliot Dole. 1949. *How to Think Creatively.* New York: Abingdon-Cokesbury Press.

Hutchison, T. W. 1977. *Knowledge and Ignorance in Economics.* Oxford: Blackwell.

———. 1981. *The Politics and Philosophy of Economics.* Oxford: Blackwell.

Jaynes, Julian. 1977. *The Origin of Consciousnesss in the Breakdown of the Bicameral Mind.* Boston: Houghton Mifflin.

Johnson, Glenn L. 1971. The quest for relevance in agricultural economics. *Am. J. Agric. Econ.* 53:728–39.

Judson, Horace Freeland. 1980. *The Search for Solutions.* New York: Holt, Rinehart, and Winston.

Keynes, John Maynard. 1936. *The General Theory of Employment, Interest, and Money.* London: Macmillan.

———. 1963. *Essays in Biography: New Edition with Three Additional Essays,* Geoffrey Keynes, ed. New York: Norton.

Koestler, Arthur. 1964. *The Act of Creation.* New York: Macmillan.

Kuhn, Thomas S. 1969. *The Structure of Scientific Revolutions,* 2nd ed. Chicago: Univ. Chicago Press.

Kuznetsov, Boris. 1979. Einstein, Science, and Culture. In A. P. French, ed., *Einstein: A Centenary Volume.* London: Heinemann.

Lancaster, Kelvin. 1971. *Consumer Demand: A New Approach.* New York: Columbia Univ. Press.

Littlefield, J. E. 1978. The mathematician's art of work. *Math. Intelligencer* 1:112–18.

Lovacs, L. 1980. A new linear programming algorithm—Better or worse than the simplex method? *Math. Intelligencer* 2:141–45.

McCloskey, Donald N. 1983. The rhetoric of economics. *J. Econ. Lit.* 21:481–517.

MacKinnon, Donald W. 1966. Instructional media in the nurturing of creativity. In Calvin W. Taylor and Frank E. Williams, *Instructional Media and Creativity,* pp. 179–216. New York: Wiley.

March, James G., and Herbert A. Simon. 1958. *Organizations.* New York: Wiley.

Maslow, Abraham H. 1967. The creative attitude. In Ross L. Mooney and Taher A. Razik, eds., *Explorations in Creativity,* pp. 43–54. New York: Harper and Row.

Maugh, Thomas H. II. 1974. Creativity: Can it be dissected? Can it be taught? *Science* 21(June):1273.

Medawar, Peter Brian. 1967. *The Art of the Soluble.* London: Methuen.

———. 1969. *Induction and Intuition in Scientific Thought.* Philadelphia: American Philosophical Society.

Middleman, Louis I., and Bruce K. Blaylock. 1983. Writing = learning: Building quantitative skills through writing. *Collegiate News and Views* 37 (fall):7-10.

Mighell, Ronald L. 1976. Offbeat reading for economic insight. *Agric. Econ. Res.* 28:120-22.

Mihram, G. Arthur. 1972. *Simulation: Statistical Foundations and Methodology.* New York: Academic Press.

Montmasson, Joseph-Marie. 1932. *Invention and the Unconscious.* Trans. by H. Stafford Hatfield. New York: Harcourt Brace.

Mosher, A. T. 1973. Higher education in the rural social sciences. *Am. J. Agric. Econ.* 55(Part II):711-19.

Muth, Richard F. 1966. Household production and consumer demand functions. *Econometrica* 34:699-708.

Myrdal, Gunnar. 1958. *Value in Social Theory.* Paul Streeten, ed. London: Routledge and Kegan Paul.

Nagel, Ernest, and James R. Newman. 1960. *Gödel's Proof.* New York: New York Univ. Press.

Nelson, George. 1970. Interview. In Stanley Rosner and Lawrence E. Abt, *The Creative Experience,* pp. 251-68. New York: Grossman.

Nietzsche, Friedrich. 1952. Composition of thus spake Zarathustra. In Brewster Ghiselin, ed., *The Creative Process,* pp. 208-11. Berkeley: Univ. California Press.

Northrop, F. C. S. 1959. *The Logic of the Sciences and Humanities.* New York: Meridian Books.

Osborn, Alex F. 1963. *Applied Imagination,* 3rd ed. New York: Scribner's.

Parnes, Sidney J. 1966. Imagination: Developed and disciplined. In Calvin W. Taylor and Frank E. Williams, eds., *Instructional Media and Creativity,* pp. 225-55. New York: Wiley.

Parnes, Sidney J., Ruth B. Noller, and Angelo M. Biondi. 1977. *Guide to Creative Action.* New York: Scribner's.

Penfield, Wilder. 1970. Interview. In Stanley Rosner and Lawrence E. Abt, *The Creative Experience,* pp. 103-14. New York: Grossman.

Piaget, Jean. 1973. *To Understand Is to Invent.* New York: Grossman.

Poincare, Henri. 1913. Mathematical creation. In *Foundations of Science,* trans. by George Bruce Halsted. New York: Science Press.

Polanyi, Michael. 1958. *Personal Knowledge.* Chicago: Univ. Chicago Press.

Polya, G. 1954a. *Induction and Analogy in Mathematics.* Vol. I, *Mathematics and Plausible Reasoning.* Princeton, N.J.: Princeton Univ. Press.

_____. 1954b. *Patterns of Plausible Inference.* Vol. II, *Mathematics and Plausible Reasoning.* Princeton, N.J.: Princeton Univ. Press.

_____. 1957. *How to Solve It: A New Aspect of Mathematical Method,* 2nd ed. Garden City, N.Y.: Doubleday.

Popper, Karl R. 1959. *The Logic of Scientific Discovery.* New York: Basic Books.

_____. 1962. *Conjectures and Refutations: The Growth of Scientific Knowledge.* New York: Basic Books.

Porterfield, Austin. 1941. *Creative Factors in Scientific Research.* Durham, N.C.: Duke Univ. Press.

Prince, George M. 1970. *The Practice of Creativity: A Manual for Dynamic Group Problem Solving.* New York: Harper and Row.

Raaheim, Kjell. 1974. *Problem Solving and Intelligence.* Bergen, Norway: Universitetsforlaget.

Rosser, J. Barkley. 1953. *Logic for Mathematicians.* New York: McGraw-Hill.

Salmon, Wesley C. 1973. Confirmation. *Sci. Am.* 228(May):75–83.

Samuelson, Paul A. 1947. *Foundations of Economic Analysis.* Cambridge, Mass.: Harvard Univ. Press.

Schultz, Theodore W. 1982. Economics and agricultural research. In Richard H. Day, ed., *Economic Analysis and Agricultural Policy,* pp. 179–91. Ames: Iowa State Univ. Press.

Schumpeter, Joseph A. 1954. *History of Economic Analysis.* Elizabeth B. Schumpeter, ed. New York: Oxford Univ. Press.

Shideler, Emerson W. 1966. *Believing and Knowing.* Ames: Iowa State Univ. Press.

Shubik, Martin. 1970. A curmudgeon's guide to microeconomics. *J. Econ. Lit.* 8:405–34.

Siegel, Barry. 1983. Baffling tale of global catastrophe. *Des Moines Sunday Register.* 28 August, pp. 1A, 3A.

Siegfried, John J. 1977. Is teaching the best way to learn? An evaluation of costs and benefits to undergraduate student proctors in elementary economics. *South. Econ. J.* 43:1394–1400.

Springer, Sally P., and Georg Deutsch. 1981. *Left Brain, Right Brain.* San Francisco: Freeman.

Stoll, Robert R. 1961. *Sets, Logic, and Axiomatic Theories.* San Francisco: Freeman.

Synge, J. L. 1951. *Science: Sense and Nonsense.* New York: W. W. Norton.

Taylor, Calvin W. 1963. Some possible relations between communication abilities and creative abilities. In Calvin W. Taylor and Frank Barron, eds., *Scientific Creativity: Its Recognition and Development,* Ch. 30. New York: Wiley.

———. 1966. Creativity through instructional media: A universe of challenges, Parts I and II. In Calvin W. Taylor and Frank E. Williams, eds., *Instructional Media and Creativity,* pp. 1–70. New York: Wiley.

Taylor, Calvin W., and Frank E. Williams, eds. 1966. *Instructional Media and Creativity.* New York: Wiley.

Tintner, Gerhard. 1974. Linear economics and the Boehm-Bawerk period of production. *Q. J. Econ.* 88:127–32.

Torrance, E. Paul. 1962. *Guiding Creative Talent.* Englewood Cliffs, N.J.: Prentice-Hall.

———. 1966. Implications of creativity research findings for instructional media. In Calvin W. Taylor and Frank E. Williams, eds., *Instructional Media and Creativity,* pp. 147–78. New York: Wiley.

Torrance, E. Paul, and R. E. Myers. 1970. *Creative Learning and Teaching.* New York: Dodd, Mead.

Toynbee, Arnold. 1964. Is America neglecting her creative minority? In Calvin W. Taylor, ed., *Widening Horizons in Creativity,* pp. 3–9. New York: Wiley.

Tulving, Endel, and Wayne Donaldson. 1972. *Organization of Memory.* New York: Academic Press.

Wallach, M., and N. Kogan. 1965. A new look at the creative-intelligence distinction. *J. Pers.* 33:348–69.

Wallas, Graham. 1926. *The Art of Thought.* New York: Harcourt Brace.

Warnock, Mary. 1976. *Imagination.* Berkeley: Univ. California Press.

Watson, James D. 1968. *The Double Helix: A Personal Account of the Discovery of the Structure of DNA.* New York: Atheneum.

Waugh, Frederick V. 1958. Alligation, forerunner of linear programming. *J. Farm Econ.* 40:89–103.

Weld, H. P. 1956. Imagination. *The Encyclopedia Americana,* vol. 14, pp. 707–8. New York: Americana Corporation.

Wiener, N. 1956. Induction. *The Encyclopedia Americana,* vol. 15, pp. 70d–73. New York: Americana Corporation.

Williams, Linda Verlee. 1983. *Teaching for the Two-Sided Mind.* Englewood Cliffs, N.J.: Prentice-Hall.

Wittrock, M. C., ed. 1977. *The Human Brain.* Englewood Cliffs, N.J.: Prentice-Hall.

Young, J. Z. 1951. *Doubt and Certainty in Science.* London: Oxford Univ. Press.

Index